The Natural World
Through Children's Literature

Recent Titles in Through Children's Literature

The Natural World Through Children's Literature

An Integrated Approach

Carol M. Butzow
and
John W. Butzow

Illustrated by Jennifer L. Rinkevich

Teacher Ideas Press, an imprint of Libraries Unlimited
Westport, Connecticut • London

Library of Congress Cataloging-in-Publication Data

Butzow, Carol M., 1942-
   The natural world through children's literature : an integrated approach / by Carol M.
   Butzow and John W. Butzow.
      p. cm. — (Through children's literature)
   Includes bibliographical references and index.
   ISBN 1-59158-351-9 (pbk : alk. paper)
   1. Nature study. 2. Children's literature in science education. I. Butzow, John W., 1939- II. Title.
   LB1532.B88   2007
   372.3'5—dc22   2006030910

British Library Cataloguing in Publication Data is available.

Library of Congress Catalog Card Number: 2006030910
ISBN: 1-59158-351-9

First published in 2007

Libraries Unlimited/Teacher Ideas Press, 88 Post Road West, Westport, CT 06881
A Member of the Greenwood Publishing Group, Inc.
www.lu.com

Printed in the United States of America

The paper used in this book complies with the
Permanent Paper Standard issued by the National
Information Standards Organization (Z39.4.8–1984).

10 9 8 7 6 5 4 3 2 1

Contents

Part 1: Living Things

Part 2: The Earth, the Atmosphere, and the Universe

Part 3: Interactions

Illustrations

Preface

Our first book, *Science Through Children's Literature*, was greeted with many positive reactions. Our idea of combining science and literature into an integrated unit was readily adaptable by numerous teachers. Our success, however, was often met by queries about when we would write for the upper grades. The result was *Intermediate Science Through Children's Literature*. Realizing that we could easily find another thirty books with science themes, we added *More Science Through Children's Literature* to our repertoire. When this volume was complete, several favorite books still had not been included. They did not center on life, earth, or physical sciences but rather were environmental in nature. These books formed the basis of *Exploring the Environment Through Children's Literature.*

A break from science topics gave us the incentive for two nonscience books that resulted in *The World of Work Through Children's Literature* and *The American Hero in Children's Literature*. Still, science was our major interest, and several months after *The American Hero* appeared we were both ready to write *The Natural World Through Children's Literature*, which is focused on observational science.

Not having a bibliography of potential volumes, we began searching lists of recent award winners for the Caldecott and the American Library Association awards. Books sounding like they would be science oriented (*What Do You Do with a Tail Like That?*) were researched over the Internet, where additional books were often found. Eventually a list of approximately forty books was established. In discussing the age level that we would target, we decided to focus on our traditional K–3 audience. We selected volumes for the youngest readers, such as *Mr. Seahorse* and *Slowly, Slowly, Slowly Said the Sloth*. More advanced topics were found in *My Bothers' Flying Machine* and the *Sea, the Storm, and the Mangrove Tangle*. Several books did not have enough science in them to be the basis of a unit. Others were too primary in nature or beyond the limits we had set.

We have organized books into the content categories of life science and earth science. Physical science was not considered as it did not fit under the umbrella of the natural world. In addition, there were books that appeared to be a combination of life and earth sciences. This third group includes such books as *Crawdad Creek* or *The Umbrella* and *The Seashore Book,* in which a location is described including both the earth and biological aspects.

Our goal in writing *The Natural World* is to present teachers with instructional alternatives focused on the science content included in excellent works of children's fiction. We intend teachers to select those activities that fit into their local curriculum and provide additional encouragement to children to become interested in and skillful with scientific concepts. We have emphasized science process skills such as observing, comparing, classifying, measuring, quantifying, and problem solving throughout our chapters.

Introduction

To be realistic, science must be experiential. Science is a process of witnessing phenomena and making up explanations and describing relationships. It must come as close to the truth as possible—avoiding the circumstances in which science is equated with the memorization of facts.

To teach science as a series of worksheets or rules is to invite many students to be ill prepared in this subject. Many students who would have enjoyed a career related to science were turned off early in their school experiences when science was presented as a set of encyclopedic facts. Our lessons use observation and related skills of comparison, contrast, and measurement as key elements of science learning. We also encourage the use of graphing, developing quantitative relationships, problem development, writing explanations of phenomena, and application to the out-of-school world as ways to extend lessons.

We present integrated units of study rather than ones that focus solely on science. By using integrated units students can greatly expand the range and applicability of their growing science knowledge. When science learnings are coupled with mathematics or other subjects, students can better appreciate the way science ideas are built up. A written sample may demand an artistic rendering to ensure that the learner is fully aware of connections between activities.

These units of study may be an adjunct to the regular curriculum or stand alone as integrated entities. Teachers are encouraged to pick and choose the activities that are most closely compatible with their objectives. They should not try to complete every activity given.

Books chosen for *The Natural World* should be read and re-read with the students. Major concepts may or may not be treated at this time. Nor should the vocabulary be given as a list to be memorized. Words are more likely to be assimilated when introduced in context.

We have chosen to present the activity list divided into disciplines: language arts, writing, social studies, science, mathematics, the arts, and information literacy. Each chapter also has a list of references and a puzzle. The puzzles are crosswords and use the vocabulary list given at the beginning of the chapter. Unless specified as a demonstration by the teacher, it is our intention that the activities be completed by the students themselves.

Part 1
Living Things

CHAPTER 1

Animal Life Cycles: *Mr. Seahorse*

Written by Eric Carle

New York: Penguin Young Readers' Group, 2004

SUMMARY

The male seahorse, who carries the female's incubating eggs in a pouch, meets other dads who care for unborn sea creatures.

RELATED CONCEPTS

Fish reproduce by laying eggs.

Fish and other animals show paternal instincts by protecting developing young.

Fish use their coloration to camouflage themselves from predators.

RELATED VOCABULARY

belly	bullhead
coral reef	hatch
Kurtus leaf	fish
lion fish	pipefish
pouch	reeds
sea weed	stickleback
stonefish	tilapia
trumpet fish	twist
wiggle	

ACTIVITIES

Language Arts

In Eric Carle's story, Mr. Seahorse has conversations with other fish. In these short dialogs, Mr. Seahorse learns a great deal about the other fish's paternal roles. This is a kind of interviewing skill. Ask the students to practice interviewing visitors to the classroom to find out information by asking a very few, carefully thought-out questions.

Re-read the book to examine the story grammar. Ask students to use the graphic organizer provided in Figure 1.1 to follow the course of the story.

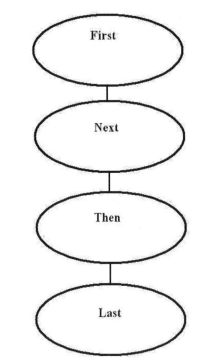

Figure 1.1. *Mr. Seahorse* **graphic organizer**

Writing

The father is the caregiver for the baby seahorses. Ask the students to name their primary caregivers. Have them write a story showing how their caregivers take care of them.

Social Studies

Seahorses live exclusively in warm waters near the equator. What seas and oceans would be home to seahorses? Name the countries along these waters.

Figure 1.2. Map of the world

Science

Although seahorses are unusually shaped fish, they have the typical fish body parts. Have children learn the parts of a fish by coloring the fish model diagram and the seahorse diagram (Figures 1.3 and 1.4).

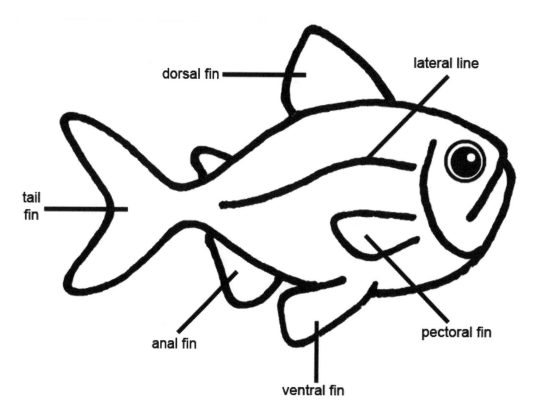

Figure 1.3. Fish diagram

Why are these animals are called seahorses? What are the defining characteristics of a seahorse? How do seahorses move?

What are the defining characteristics of fish and other ocean creatures?

Land animals also are known to tend their babies—for example, the wolf, the gibbon, the ostrich, the pygmy marmoset, the flamingo, and the mallard. Compare these animals to the seahorse.

Mathematics

Look up the length of other sea creatures that the students know. Make a line graph to compare the size of these animals to the seahorse.

Seahorses are approximately 1.5 to 12 inches in height. Find other objects in the classroom to help visualize the size of this animal, such as a class book or a TV remote.

Metric measurement can also be used to find objects equivalent to the size of a seahorse, which would be between 4 and 30 centimeters.

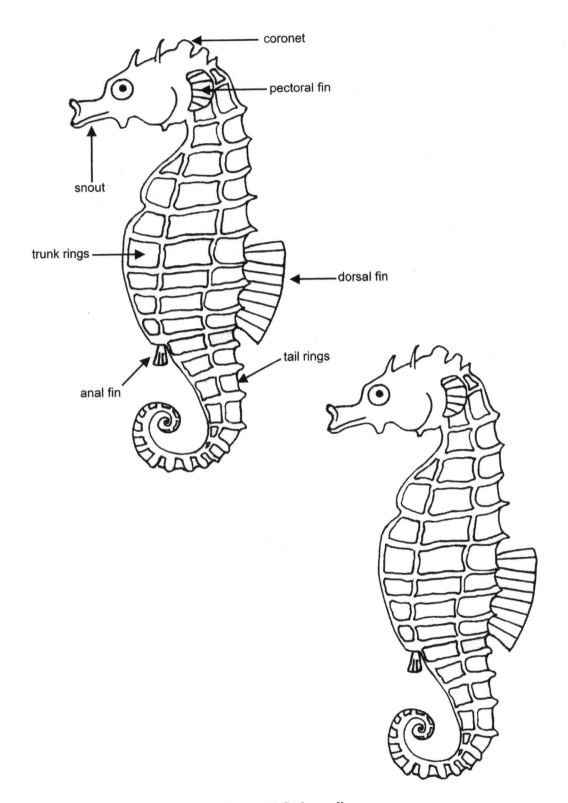

Figure 1.4. Seahorse diagram

The Arts

Draw various examples of seaweed, especially those that are edible. Does anyone have a recipe for seaweed soup?

Use variegated construction paper to make the outline of a seahorse. Paste this to blue paper and decorate it with other ocean plants and animals, especially seaweed.

Information Literacy

Have the students research other fathers who tend their babies—for example, the stickleback, the tilapia, pipefish, the Kurtus, or nursery fish. How are these animals alike and different?

What are the needs of a human baby? How can human fathers help to tend them?

REFERENCES

http://www.pbs.org/wgbh/nova/seahorse/. The life cycle of the seahorse.

Another book that describes how male animals help raise young is

Collard, Sneed B., III. *Animal Dads*. New York: Houghton Mifflin, 1997.

Mr. Seahorse

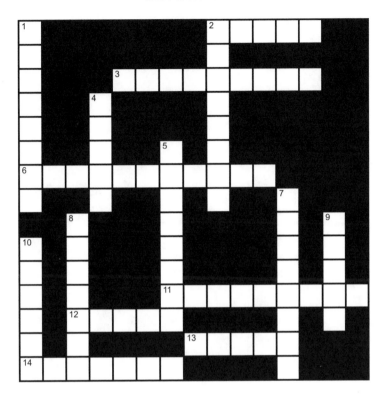

Across

2. The bulging or rounded part of the body.
3. Coral animals grow together to form this hiding place.
6. Builds the nest and cares for the eggs
11. A reddish brown fish that hides behind rocks.
12. A bag like structure on an animal's body
13. Grass like water plants.
14. Plants that grow in the water

Down

1. A coral reef fish with spiky fins
2. A fish with barbs on its head that guards its young.
4. To come out of an egg.
5. A fish that is colored and shaped like a leaf
7. A slender straight fish similar to the seahorse
8. The male fish holds eggs of developing fish in its mouth.
9. To turn around and around.
10. A nursery fish—holds its young on a hook on its head

CHAPTER 2

Animal Movement: *From Head to Toe*

Written by Eric Carle

New York: HarperCollins, 1997

SUMMARY

Young children follow the movements of selected animals.

RELATED CONCEPTS

Animals and humans move in similar ways.

Movement is always with reference to prior position, for example, up versus down.

RELATED VOCABULARY

arch	arms
bend	chest
clap	feet
hands	hips
kick	knees
legs	neck
raise	shoulders
stomp	thump
toes	turn
wave	wiggle

ACTIVITIES

Language Arts

What animal am I? Play a game of Twenty Questions based on animals in the book.

Eric Carle authored more than seventy books and has over forty currently in print. Select some of these works to share with the students. *Slowly, Slowly, Slowly Said the Sloth* and *Mr. Seahorse* are featured in this book. *A House for Hermit Crab* and *The Grouchy Ladybug* are also about movement. More information about Eric Carle is available through his Web page at http://www.eric-carle.com/books.html.

Writing

Have students write about and illustrate their favorite way of moving— playing softball, running, gymnastics, dancing, jumping rope, exercises, etc.

Select an animal from the book and write about the way it moves. An illustration can accompany this.

Social Studies

Find the environment in which each animal in the book lives. Mark these countries on the world map (see Chapter 1 for the world map). Where do most animals live? What continents have the least number of animals?

Are there students from other cultures in the school? Are their movements and gestures the same as ours—waving, greeting an old friend, saying goodnight to parents, indicating disapproval, speaking to a teacher, cheering on a sports team, etc.?

Science

Watch the movements of various animals using video cameras. Or study the movement of family pets. How are they similar to humans? How are they different?

Read this book and allow students to pantomime the gestures being shown. After several readings of the book, the students should be ready to follow a dance routine that will contain some of these movements—turn head, raise shoulder, bend knees, wiggle hips, etc. A physical education teacher or parent may be able to choreograph the routine or dance.

As human beings we have many joints—for example, shoulders, hips, elbows, wrists, knees, and ankles. Use the skeleton illustration (Figure 2.1) to locate the joints of the human body. How are these joints important to the body? Can one move without using joints? What happens if a joint is injured?

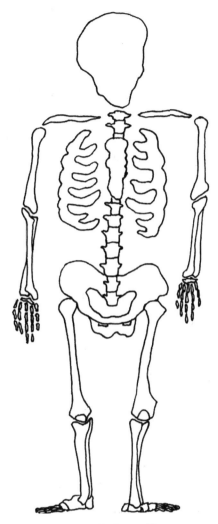

Figure 2.1. Skeleton diagram

Playing the *Twister* game entails much physical movement as well as fun.
Have relay races.

Mathematics

This book is about movement. How far can students throw an object such as a beanbag? How far can they kick a ball during a game of kickball? How far can they run in ten seconds, etc.? Make predictions, then see how close you are to the actual measurement.

Sequence the size of the animals in the book by length or by body weight. Research will be needed to find these numbers.

The Arts

Eric Carle used much finger painting and collage in his illustrations. Have the students cut up small pieces of construction paper to form a picture that can be mounted onto a finger painting they have done.

Play a game of Simon Says. All of the motions should come from the book—turn head, raise shoulders, thump chest, bend knees, etc.

Information Literacy

Animals move in many different ways depending on where they live and what they are trying to do. Research the movements of animals within their environment. Ask students to work in groups based on whether the animal lives on the land, in the air, in the water, or under the water. Develop lists of verbs describing the unique movements of specific animals.

REFERENCES

Carle, Eric. *The Art of Eric Carle*. New York: Philomel Books, 1996. This is a book of essays and selections from Mr. Carle's art.

Carle, Eric. *The Grouchy Ladybug*. New York: HarperCollins, 1977.

Carle, Eric. *A House for Hermit Crab*. Saxonville, MA: Picture Book Studio, 1987.

From Head to Toe

Across

3. To move upward.
6. The upper limbs of a person.
8. The longest part of the body.
10. Located at the front end of the feet.
11. You wave good-bye with these.
13. To beat one's chest.
14. Holds the head onto the chest.
16. To make a noise with one's hands or paws.
18. The part of the body containing the heart and lungs.

Down

1. You put shoes on these.
2. To move repeatedly from side to side.
4. To make repeated up and down movements.
5. Joints in the middle of the legs.
7. To move a body part from one direction to another.
9. Joints connecting the arms to the body.
10. To twist in another direction.
11. The top of the legs.
12. To make a noise with the foot on the ground.
15. To move a foot through the air.
17. To make into a curved shape.

From *The Natural World Through Children's Literature: An Integrated Approach* by Carol M. Butzow and John W. Butzow. Westport, CT: Libraries Unlimited/Teacher Ideas Press. Copyright © 2007.

CHAPTER 3

Birds and Bird Behavior: *Wild Birds*

Written by Joanne Ryder
New York: HarperCollins, 2003

SUMMARY

A girl carefully observes birds during several seasons around the house and near the bird feeder.

RELATED CONCEPTS

Wild birds live in many different places in the environment.

Wild birds typically feed and care for their young.

Birds use their feathers to help them fly and also as insulation against cold.

Bird feeders require careful maintenance and proper choice of food.

Wild birds are easy to identify based on size, shape, color, method of flying, and choice of habitat.

RELATED VOCABULARY

blue jay	oriole
blue martin	pileated woodpecker
cardinal	purple finch
cedar waxwing	redwinged blackbird
chickadee	robin
crow	rosebrested grosbeak
goldfinch	scarlet tanager
hummingbird	sparrow
indigo bunting	starling
junco	

ACTIVITIES

Language Arts

As the teacher reads the book, have the students pantomime the actions of the wild birds—for example, gliding, swooping, and looping. What other words can be used to describe these actions?

Joanne Ryder, the author of this book, has written many books with science themes for youngsters. Select other books of hers to read. Compare these books to each other.

This book focuses on the characteristics of common birds found in bird guides. Students should be able to identify several birds from their area. This includes learning the size of the bird, its physical description and color, its behavior, where it nests, what it eats, and whether it is migratory. These attributes, as well as a silhouette of the bird, can be displayed on a bulletin board.

Writing

Why do people enjoy watching birds—for example, being a bird watcher, recording the sounds of the birds, maintaining a bird feeder, feeding birds in a park? Give specific examples of when you have watched birds.

Observe how birds fly, walk, or hop. Have students write short descriptions like those in Joanna Ryder's book of how different kinds of birds appear as they move.

Social Studies

When birds fly south for the winter they follow certain paths called flyways. Over which states are these flyways to be found? Are these flyways in the vicinity of the students' homes?

Science

Feathers on birds are also referred to as their plumage. Why are some birds so brilliantly colored while others are quite dull? Why do birds have feathers?

Find out which birds are indigenous to your local area. Which birds will fly south for the winter? Which ones will continue to live in the same locale? If at all possible, participate as a class in the Great Backyard Bird Count, which is often held in February. Its Web site furnishes a checklist of birds for your state, province, or region (http://gbbc.birdsource.org/gbbcApps/checklist).

There are nineteen birds pictured and named on the publication page of *Wild Birds*. These include many that can be found during the winter bird count in northern states, as well as in warmer parts of the United States. If you are able to keep a bird feeder near a classroom window or in a place where children can observe it daily, keep a daily log of the number of each kind of bird that is observed. Note the size of each bird and if possible which bird seed the bird prefers.

Many of the birds selected by Joanne Ryder for her book are included in lists of birds that naturalists and educators believe children should be able to recognize. One renowned book is *Birds That Every Child Should Know* by Neltje Blanchan, which was published in 1907. This wonderful book of nature lore is still available online at http://www.kellscraft.com/ECSKBirds/ECSKBirdscontent.html.

To sprout birdseed, take a moist kitchen sponge and lay it on a plate. Sprinkle about a tablespoon of birdseed on the sponge. Keep the sponge moist. In a few days, the seeds will germinate.

NOTE: If you do begin feeding birds and it becomes very cold out, it is a good idea to be sure that someone fills the bird feeder regularly during school vacations and periods when school is closed for several days.

Birds are important to the reproduction of certain plants. Explain the relationship between their eating of seeds and the plants that grow in the area. What other animals help to transport seeds?

If it is not possible for students to see live birds in their vicinity, the use of Web cams is beneficial. Or visit a zoo or aviary. Some birding Web cams have been identified by the Cornell University Birdhouse Network at http://www.birds.cornell.edu/birdhouse2/nestboxcam/.

Mathematics

Keep a frequency count of the birds observed from the classroom bird feeder. Rank order the birds from the most frequently seen to the least. Make charts to illustrate your findings.

Keep track of the quantity of bird seed consumed each week. If food preferences were observed, make a chart depicting these.

The Arts

Describe the features that distinguish a bird from other groups of animals such as insects, mammals, amphibians, reptiles, and fish. Have students draw sketches of existing birds or invent birds using their imagination.

Draw birds to the size that they exist in reality—for example, a hummingbird is about 3½ inches long, a robin is 9 to 11 inches long, a woodpecker is about 8½ to 9½ inches long. Sequence the birds by size on the bulletin board or in a mobile. A very good reference book is *Feathers for Lunch* by Lois Ehlert.

Younger children may wish to color the coloring book page of nine common winter birds (Figure 3.1) to help to learn identification skills.

Figure 3.1. Bird coloring pages

Obtain plans or craft kits to construct and maintain a bird feeder near the school (see Figure 3.2).

Figure 3.2. Bird feeder

Information Literacy

Have the class use the Internet to obtain information about a favorite bird. Print out pictures, descriptions of feeding, and nesting behavior as well as something unusual about the bird. Some children will want to learn about birds with unusual names such as the "booby," "frigate bird," "flycatcher," etc.

REFERENCES

Arnold, Carolyn. *Birds: Natures Magnificent Flying Machines*. Watertown MA: Charlesbridge Publishing, 2003.

Ehlert, Lois. *Feathers for Lunch*. New York: Harcourt, 1996.

Latimer, Jonathan, Karen Stray Nolting, and Roger Tory Peterson. *Backyard Birds for Young Naturalists*. New York: Houghton Mifflin, 1996.

Peterson, Roger Tory. *Birds of Eastern and Central North America, Fifth Edition*. Edited by Virginia Peterson. New York: Houghton Mifflin, 2002.

Peterson, Roger Tory. *Feeder Birds: Eastern North America*. Edited by Virginia Peterson. New York: Houghton Mifflin, 2000.

Ryder, Joanne. *One Small Fish*. New York: Morrow Junior Books, 1993.

Ryder, Joanne. *Winter Whale*. New York: Morrow Junior Books, 1991.

Wild Birds

Across

2. A strawberry red bird with brown wings and tail.
5. A small grey bird with rust colored cap and back.
8. A bird with grey back, white belly, and a black cap.
9. Bright red bird with black around base of beak.
11. A slate grey bird with white outer feathers.
13. A bird that is blue above, with wings and tail mixed with black.

Down

1. A bright yellow bird with black cap and wings.
3. The largest swallow, purple with a notched tail.
4. A bird with warm brown wings and a black mask.
5. A large glossy black bird with little white splotches.
6. A brilliant orange bird with black head and back.
7. A big bully of a blue, black, and white bird.
10. A brown bird with brick red underparts.
12. A large black bird that says "caw, caw."

CHAPTER **4**

Animal Anatomy:
What Do You Do with a Tail Like This?

Written by Steve Jenkins and Robin Page

Boston: Houghton Mifflin, 2003

SUMMARY

Unique aspects of several animals are portrayed in a guessing game format.

RELATED CONCEPTS

Various animals use their tails, eyes, ears, mouth, and feet in unique ways.

Animal species have made a vide variety of adaptations to their environments.

RELATED VOCABULARY

ear	mouth
eye	nose
feet	tail

ACTIVITIES

Language Arts

Read the book to the students, reviewing the animals that they know. Compare these animals with the drawings of the completed animals in the information section at the end of the book.

Use an animal encyclopedia or file of animal photos to select unknown animals that have unique characteristics. Share these in small groups.

Assign each student an animal. Draw a picture of the animal's tail. Play a game of Pin the Tail on the Donkey. Which "tail" is the winner?

Compare this book with another one by the same author—*What Do You Do When Something Wants to Eat You?* Notice the various media used for the illustrations.

Writing

Make up tall tales or fantasy stories that explain how various animals were created—for example, how the raccoon got its tail, how the goat got its horns, how the cheetah got its spots, etc.

Social Studies

Different parts of the body distinguish animals from each other. The earth has many kinds of landforms that distinguish countries and continents. These landforms include mountains, mesas, plateaus, hills, valleys, deserts, lakes, etc. Using relief maps, analyze the landforms that distinguish countries and continents. Have each student draw a picture to show one landform—for example, people skiing on a mountain.

Identify animals that are indigenous to each continent (use the world map from Chapter 1).

Science

Why do animals have different tails, mouths, eyes, ears, and feet? Discuss the word "adaptation" in connection with this question. How have humans adapted to their situation?

Place animals in their biological groups—for example, mammals, fish, birds, amphibians, reptiles, and birds. Are there similarities and differences among the groups?

Have the students invent an animal and draw the environment to which it adapts itself.

Why do animals have tails? Brainstorm this question before giving the students answers; for example, animals have tails for balance, to fix themselves to a tree, to move, to communicate, to show emotion, to rid themselves of insects, to keep warm, and to find direction.

Mathematics

The following numbers are indicative of the number of species found in each biological group of animals. Practice reading the numbers, then put them in descending order starting with insects. A graph can be made from these data. Ask each other questions about the data—for example, which group is the largest? Are there more bird or fish species?

Insects	920,000 species
Mammals	4,260 species
Reptiles	8,100 species
Birds	10,000 species
Amphibians	5,383 species
Fish	27,000 species

NOTE: Numbers can be rounded off for younger learners.

The Arts

Have the students make a self-portrait, which can be cut up into four sections. Reassemble the drawing with those of three other students. What appear to be the outstanding characteristics by which the students can be identified?

Construct animals using materials that are very distinctive—for example, felt, fake fur, corduroy, wool, cotton, feathers, or contact paper. Share the animals and discuss their unique qualities.

Information Literacy

Challenge the class to learn more about one of the animals in the book or other animals that hold a special interest for the students. Select animals such as the bat, jackrabbit, mole, elephant, hyena, etc., and answer the questions below using reference books in the library media center or the Internet.

On which continent does this animal live?

What is the climate like where this animal lives?

What does the animal eat?

What is unusual about this animal?

What unusual characteristics help the animal survive?

If you could talk to an animal, what would you like to ask it?

REFERENCES

Introduce children to these other books by Steve Jenkins for additional opportunities to learn how animals differ in their adaptations to the environment.

Jenkins, Steve. *Big and Little*. Boston: Houghton Mifflin, 1996.

Jenkins, Steve. *Biggest, Strongest, Fastest*. Boston: Houghton Mifflin, 1995.

Jenkins, Steve. *What Do You Do When Something Wants to Eat You*? Boston: Houghton Mifflin, 1997.

Page, Robin, and Steve Jenkins. *Animals in Flight*. New York: Houghton Mifflin, 2001.

What Do You Do with a Tail Like This?

Across

3. Can breathe with its nose extended out of the water.
4. Can chase away flies with its tail.
6. Can capture insects with its long tongue.

Down

1. Can eat with its feet.
2. Can find objects with its special hearing.
5. Can see prey from high in the air.

CHAPTER 5

Life of Insects: *The Very Ugly Bug*

Written by Liz Pinchon
Wilton, CT: Little Tiger Press, 2004

SUMMARY

A bug thinks she is ugly and tries to disguise herself. Unfortunately she makes herself more attractive to her enemies, and she can't wait to return to her old self.

RELATED CONCEPTS

Animals have evolved a variety of methods to blend into or stand out from the environment.

In protective coloration, the camouflaged prey animals are difficult for predators to see.

Camouflage can be color related, shade related, or shape related (mimicry).

Warning coloration is the opposite of protective coloration; a bright color often signals that the prey is poisonous or bad tasting to the predator.

RELATED VOCABULARY

abdomen	mimicry
antenna	predator
camouflage	prey
head	protective coloration
legs	thorax
warning coloration	wings

ACTIVITIES

Language Arts

Have the students use the graphic in Figure 5.1 to examine the story of the ugly bug.

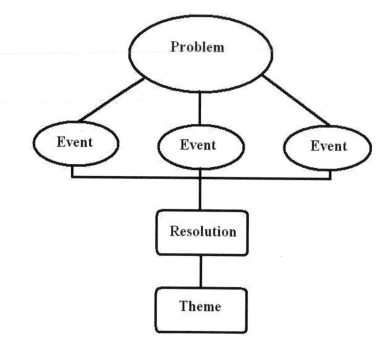

Figure 5.1. *Ugly Bug* graphic organizer

A story about a lion that wished to change his looks to impress his friends is *Dandelion* by Don Freeman. Compare him to the ugly bug. How do people try to look more beautiful?

Using a thesaurus, find other words that mean "ugly" and "beautiful." How could you use these in a story, for example, a fairy tale?

Writing

How could you convince the "ugly" bug that she was really quite beautiful? Use many descriptive words.

What makes an insect ugly? Is it the head, the eyes, the back, the legs, the wings? Certainly this is what the ugly bug thought. Write a description of an insect to prove that it is ugly, or to prove that you think insects are nice looking. NOTE: Students may wish to look at insects on the Internet or in a field guide before writing.

Insects usually are depicted as useless and contemptible. This does not parallel the situation of the ugly bug or other insects in children's literature. Look at things from another point of view and have students write a positive poem about an insect. For example:

> *Once there was a little bug,*
> *His mother put him on the rug,*
> *He cried and cried, until his eyes were dried,*
> *All he needed was a hug.*

Social Studies

Draw a map or diagram of the ugly bug's house. What rooms would it have? What would it look like? Are their other bugs living nearby?

Science

Find out from local authorities (such as the local county office of the state university's cooperative extension service) which insects are most common in the area where the students reside. Are these insects a problem to the community? How can they be controlled? Are there insects that perform a positive service to humans?

In some cases, insects are very helpful to humans because they cross-pollinate plants, eat other insects that are harmful, and serve as a food source in many countries.

Why are most insects considered to be pests or plagues? What do they do to deserve their reputation?

Have the class learn the major parts of an insect's (bug's) body. The head (eyes, antennae, mouth parts)and the thorax (wings, six legs, and the abdomen) make up the typical bug's anatomy. Use the illustration of a bug to invent colorful or camouflaged examples (Figure 5.2).

Figure 5.2. Insect diagram

Divide the class into small groups. Provide each group of students with a specific number of brightly colored, small objects such as red, green, and yellow paper clips. Challenge students to select their fastest paper clip "picker-upper." Try picking up paper clips of a specific color against a background of white paper. Do this for a short time, such as ten seconds. Now try the same activity with green or yellow or red paper as the background. Is there a relationship between the color of the background and the color of the paper clips?

NOTE: When the color of the clips and the color of the background match, a camouflage situation has been created.

Mathematics

If every generation of insects produced ten individuals that lived to maturity, how many generations would it take to reach one million?

What is the cost to make a Styrofoam insect as described in the arts section? There are three 3½-inch foam balls for each insect at 50 cents each, one-third of a package of pipe cleaners at 89 cents per package, and two wiggly eyes at 5 cents each. NOTE: Some craft stores have oval Styrofoam balls to be used for the abdomen. Also, some stores carry black Styrofoam balls.

Estimate how many bugs are shown on the inside page of the cover and the back page.

The Arts

Insects can be made from Styrofoam balls, pipe cleaners, and wiggly eyes. For each insect, students will need three black Styrofoam balls—one for the head, onto which they will place two eyes and two antennae; one for the thorax, which houses six legs and one or two sets of wings; and one for the abdomen. Legs, wings, and antennae are made from black pipe cleaners, and wiggly eyes can be purchased in a craft store. To make the insect "ugly," add pieces of cloth, felt, ribbon, etc.

Insects or flowers, similar to those on the inside cover of the book, can be made by pressing a thumb on an inkpad and then placing it on a sheet of paper. Add legs and antennae or flower petals to the thumbprint to produce an insect or a flower.

Information Literacy

Challenge students to find examples of protective and warning coloration from reference books and Web sites. Print pictures of example animals for a colorful bulletin board display.

REFERENCES

Zim, Herbert S., and Clarence Cottam. *Insects, Revised Edition*. New York: A Golden Guide from St. Martin's Press, 2001.

The Very Ugly Bug

Across

5. Coloring that tells the predator that the prey is not good to eat.
6. Insects have six of these.
7. Gets caught by the predator.
8. Colors or patterns that hide an insect.
9. The middle segment of an insect.
11. The last segment of an insect's body.

Down

1. Pretending to be someone or something else.
2. Insects fly away with these.
3. Stick out from the head of an insect.
4. Coloring that helps the prey from being seen.
7. The hunter that catches the prey.
10. The segment containing the mouth and eyes.

CHAPTER 6

Animals of the Rainforest:
Slowly, Slowly, Slowly Said the Sloth

Written by Eric Carle

New York: Penguin Putnam Books for Young Children, 2002

SUMMARY

The sloth explains his sedentary way of living to the other rainforest animals.

RELATED CONCEPTS

Sloths conserve energy by living a very quiet lifestyle.

Sloths are dependent on the conservation of rainforests for their existence.

Sloths and other animals are uniquely adapted to living in the rainforest.

RELATED VOCABULARY

anaconda	peccary
armadillo	puma
caiman	quetzal
coati	tapir
jaguar	toucan
macaw	

ACTIVITIES

Language Arts

The Amazon animals made fun of the sloth because he was slow and different from them. Just as animals are different, so are people. Ask students how they carry out the following tasks. Are there differences?

Making a sandwich

Celebrating a birthday

Selecting a movie or television show to watch

Getting dressed in the morning

Going to school

The teacher should select eight to ten of the words from the sloth's speech for the children to learn. Try to use these in conversation during the day.

Read several of Eric Carle's books, especially those about movement—for example, *From Head to Toe, The Grouchy Ladybug*.

Jane Goodall, who wrote an introduction for this book, is an expert on primates. Have someone read her words and have the class discuss them.

Writing

The sloth said that he was "slow, quiet and boring." Have the students describe themselves and the things they like. This might be done as an acrostic—for example,

A—attractive person

N—novel reader

N—nice personality

E—excellent swimmer

Select an animal from the array shown at the end of the book. Research the animal in an encyclopedia or the Internet. Write a short description of the animal using the information you have learned.

Have the students write a fictional tale about their animal in the manner of *Slowly, Slowly, Slowly Said the Sloth*. Post all of the stories on a bulletin board or on a hallway display.

The sloth is a very unique animal. People are unique as well. Have the students break into pairs. Have each student write what is unique about his or her partner. Share these with the class.

Many people want to develop the rain forest for commercial purposes. Do we really need a rain forest? Must the animals who live there be protected? Would the indigenous tribes not be better in a more civilized environment? What effects does destroying the rain forest have on the planet's climates? Have a debate between developers and those who want to preserve this large area.

Social Studies

What are the characteristics of a rainforest? Locate ten or more rainforests throughout the world (see Figure 6.1). What is the climate like in each of these locations? What adaptations do animals need to make to live there?

Rainforest boundary

Figure 6.1 Rainforest map

NOTE: See the map of the world in Chapter 1.

What could happen to rainforest animals if the rainforests continue to be devastated by overcutting of wild hardwoods such as mahogany?

Science

Mother and baby sloth photographs can be found at http://tropicaltreefarms.com/htm/main/photos/mother_and_baby_sloth.jpg. Mother sloths care for their young and teach them to forage for food. How do other animals help their young survive?

Sloths eat tree leaves and are classified as herbivores. Jaguars eat meat and are carnivores. Peccaries are omnivores because they eat mostly roots, fruit, and other plant materials but also eat insects and rodents. Make a list of animals the children know and list their eating preferences. Are they herbivores, carnivores, or omnivores?

Sloths live in a very damp environment and have hairs adapted to allow green colored algae (colonies of one celled organisms) on their bodies. Algae can grow almost anywhere where it is relatively warm and moist. In the fall and spring, look outside the school building on rocks and other places for signs of algae.

Sloths live in the tops of the rain forest trees and eat leaves. They conserve their individual energy by being active only about 20 percent of the time. Ask the class to compare the sloth to themselves. What do they use energy to do? What does the sloth use energy to do?

Mathematics

Using a circular protractor, measure out 270 degrees—the distance the sloth can turn its head. How far can the human head turn? What additional items could you see in your classroom if your head could turn farther?

Practice measuring angles—for example, 45 degrees, 60 degrees, 180 degrees, 360 degrees. How many degrees around is the earth?

Sequence the animals in the book by length.

The Arts

The Amazon rainforest is the largest one on earth. Research some tribes from the Amazon and learn about their arts and crafts at Web sites such as http://www.amazonartsandcrafts.com/, which provides information about the Amazon Indians. The key words "Amazon Rainforest arts and crafts" will also supply much information.

Information Literacy

Look for Journey into Amazonia on your public broadcasting channel. It is a series of programs about exploring the region's plants, animals, and ecological conditions (http://www.pbs.org/journeyintoamazonia/about.html).

REFERENCES

Carle, Eric. *From Head to Toe*. New York: HarperCollins, 1997.

Carle, Eric. *The Grouchy Ladybug*. New York: HarperCollins, 1977

Cherry, Lynne. *The Great Kapok Tree*. San Diego: Harcourt Brace Jovanovich, 1990.

Slowly, Slowly, Slowly Said the Sloth

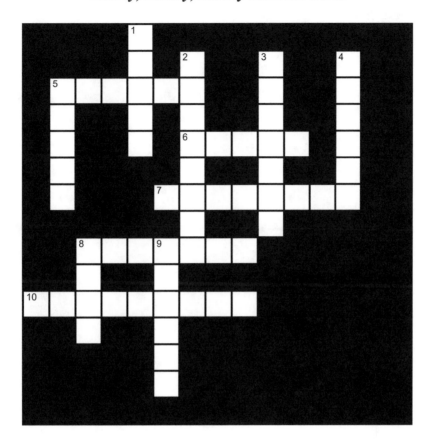

Across

5. A bird with a large yellow bill.
6. A member of the raccoon family.
7. It has a two-foot-long tongue.
8. A pig-like animal.
10. A mammal that has bony plates for protection.

Down

1. Large bird resembling a parrot.
2. The largest known snake in the world.
3. An intense green rain forest bird with long tail feathers.
4. A large spotted cat.
5. It has a long nose and is related to rhinos.
8. The rainforest mountain lion.
9. A smaller member of the crocodile family.

CHAPTER 7

Freshwater Life:
In the Small, Small Pond

Written by Denise Fleming
New York: Henry Holt, 1993

SUMMARY

A child's observation of pond life is described in verse.

RELATED CONCEPTS

Pond animals depend on other animals for food.

Pond animals have specialized adaptations for movement and sensation.

Many of the animals in the pond hibernate during the winter.

RELATED VOCABULARY

black duck	minnow
crayfish	muskrat
dragonfly	raccoon
frog	swallow
goose	turtle
heron	whirligig beetle

ACTIVITIES

Language Arts

Have children each select one of the animals in the pond to describe. They should include as many verbs as possible describing the actions of the animal, as well as ways that animals use their legs, wings, fins, etc.

Try doing this activity twice, once before a visit to a pond and again after the visit.

Writing

As a follow-up to the fieldwork suggested in the science section, have the children write about the pond they visited or would like to visit. Emphasize all of the things that can be observed in the pond environment. Emphasize what is personally observed.

Social Studies

On a map of the local area, for example, a county map, locate and count the number of small lakes, ponds, and reservoirs in the area. Did people construct them for a specific purpose, or are they natural bodies of water? Does a local group, company, or governmental group, such as a county parks commission, care for any of these bodies of water? Write to the owner or custodian of these bodies of water for information about potential field sites.

Sometimes a pond can serve as a breeding ground for unwelcome insects like mosquitoes. Which insect pests are common in the area where the students live? What dangers do they carry? By what means can these pests be eliminated?

Science

Organize a class visit to a small local pond. One in a nature park or on a farm is preferable if it has a water depth less than four feet. It is best to make the visit in the fall or spring for residents of northern climates. Be sure to bring at least one adult for every three children to ensure that everyone behaves in a proper and safe manner.

Children tend to be noisy and scare away animals when approaching a pond. Carefully rehearse the rules for the visit:

Be quiet, talk only in a whisper.

Stay with your adult leader.

Keep track of the animals you see, noting especially where the animals are in the pond and what the animals are doing.

Back in the classroom make a bulletin board or other large pictorial record of the animals observed. Emphasize the actions of the animals.

If a visit to a pond is impossible, an alternate method is to make a video visit to a local pond. Educator organizations also provide information about ponds in a number of locations throughout the world. See, for example, http://www.uen.org/utahlink/pond/.

Students should look for answers to the following questions about the animals they saw:

How does the animal move?

What does the animal eat?

How does it avoid being caught?

Does it have some kind of camouflage to avoid being seen?

The teacher or a parent volunteer should collect samples of pond water in a closed container. Have the students gently shake the bottle and then place it on a table. The water will settle out in layers. Have the students identify each layer. NOTE: Be sure to gather a bit of the pond bottom when collecting the sample.

Mathematics

While at the pond, make measurements of the length and width of the pond using a measurement wheel. Make a general sketch of notable items around the pond with measurements of their locations as well. Back in the classroom using graph paper or a large graph grid drawn on a very large sheet of paper, make a map or series of maps of the pond based on your measurements (see Figure 7.1).

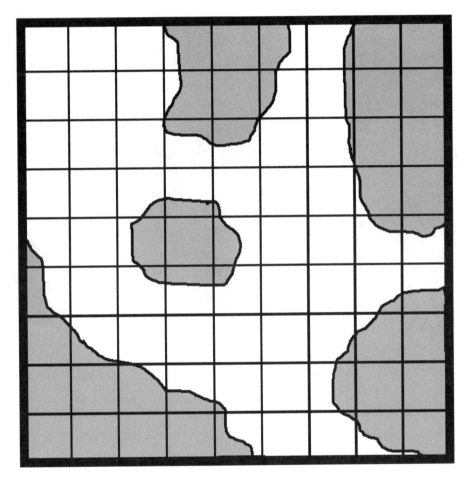

Figure 7.1. Pond map

The Arts

Make cutouts of the animals that live near or in the pond (See Figure 7.3). Make a large outline of the cross section of the pond to display the cutouts (see Figure 7.2)—for example, the snapping turtles live at the bottom, fish live in the middle or on top of the pond, insects live on or above the surface of the pond.

Figure 7.2. Animal silhouettes

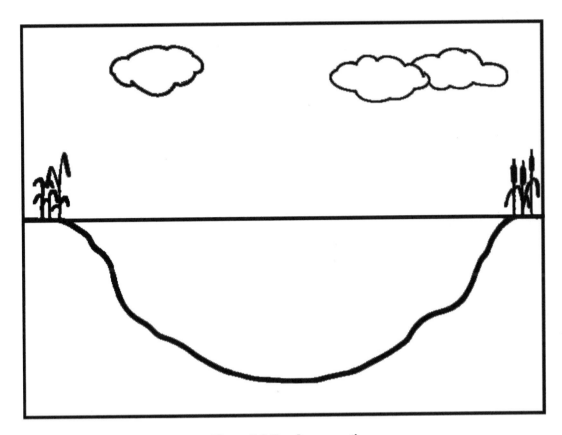

Figure 7.3. Pond cross section

Study the body of a dragonfly. Re-create this insect with construction paper and place it at the top of the pond on the bulletin board.

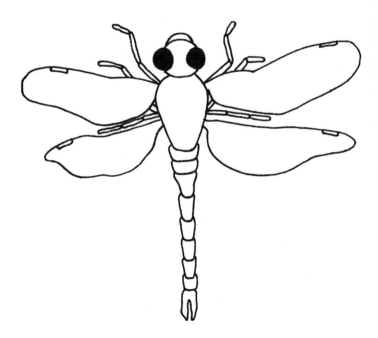

Figure 7.4. Dragonfly diagram

Information Literacy

Many professionals are engaged in pond studies or limnology. Ask the students to use the Internet to discover examples of the areas of interest of these specialists. One Web site that lists many links is http://www.limnology.org/links.html.

REFERENCES

Reid, George K. *Pond Life*. rev. ed. New York: Golden Guides from St. Martin's Press, 2001. This is an excellent reference for children that provides details about the pond's ecological structure, seasonal changes, and information about specific plants and animals.

In the Small, Small Pond

Across

3. A crustacean that looks like a small lobster.
5. A small fish such as a chub or dace.
6. An amphibian that has long jumping legs.
7. A long slender-billed bird that feeds on fish and frogs.
9. A bird that feeds by "tipping up" to get its head under water.
10. A reptile with a shell into which it can withdraw its legs and head.
11. A bird that nests on pond banks and skims the water to drink.

Down

1. A large flying insect with two sets of horizontal wings.
2. This insect uses its paddle-like legs to skim over the surface of the water.
4. A large bird that flies in a v-formation.
5. A fur-bearing animal that burrows into the bank and stores up plants to eat later.
8. A fur-bearing animal with a ringed tail that eats fish, frogs, and crayfish.

From *The Natural World Through Children's Literature: An Integrated Approach* by Carol M. Butzow and John W. Butzow. Westport, CT: Libraries Unlimited/Teacher Ideas Press. Copyright © 2007.

CHAPTER 8

Animal Adaptation and Survival:
Teeth, Tails, and Tentacles

Written by Christopher Wormell

Philadelphia: Running Press, 2004

SUMMARY

This animal counting book features many different mammals, reptiles, birds, fish, amphibians, and invertebrates.

RELATED CONCEPTS

Animals differ by size, shape, number of limbs, and ability to move.

Animals have a variety of adaptations to help them survive.

Animals have adaptations to help them move about in specific environments.

RELATED VOCABULARY

abdomen	paddles
antenna	scales
antlers	shell
claws	skin
feathers	snout
fins	tail
flukes	tooth
fur	tentacles
head	thorax
hoof	trunk
horns	tube feet
humps	tusks
legs	wings

ACTIVITIES

Language Arts

Make each day a special day by featuring one animal and one number—for example, "Today is brought to you by the rhinoceros and the number 1." Learn about this animal before moving onto the camel and number 2.

Many animal names have unexpected plural forms—other than the plural formed by adding an "s" to the singular noun. Some animals such as deer or elk use the same word for both singular and plural. The plural for fish is either fish or fishes, but the plural of starfish is starfish. Encourage your students to work with their dictionaries to look up the singular and plural forms of the animals they study in this unit and other subjects. Have them make and label pictures of animals singularly and in groups.

Writing

Write a story about an invented animal such as a "hippogator" that has a peculiar adaptation. The "hippogator," for example, has a head of a hippopotamus and a tail of an alligator. It is especially well adapted to living in tropical ponds and eating a great deal of plant material but it can still lash out with its armored tail when attacked.

Invent another "two-creature" animal from the unit. Tell why you like this creature.

Social Studies

Animal names change depending upon where one lives. The American elk or wapiti is called (stag) red deer in England. The same is true for the European and Asiatic reindeer, which is called caribou in North America.

What are the ways that people relate to animals within their culture? How do they use animal images as part of holiday celebrations? Some examples are Santa Claus's reindeer, the Easter bunny, Punxsutawney Phil, and Paul Bunyan's blue ox in North American culture.

Other animals are shunned because of religious restrictions or are part of celebrations—for example, the lamb in Jewish rituals.

Science

Each of the animals in the book has a specific adaptation that helps it survive. The (stag) red deer's antlers are a means of defense, while the chameleon's changeable color helps provide camouflage. Ask the children to identify the adaptations and the ways each adaptation assists the animal to survive.

Create challenge cards for the children to respond to in identifying animals and their habitat. Some examples follow:

Name an animal with a large nose that can shoot water.

Name an animal that has a hairy mane on its head.

Name an animal that has very large, flattened antlers.

Name an animal that has a flattened snout.

Name an animal that has only one horn.

NOTE: The challenge cards may include any animal known to the children, not just the ones in the book.

Mathematics

Using math manipulatives, have students figure out the answers to these problems.

I see sixteen legs. How many camels are there?

I see twenty feet. How many chameleons are there?

There are two octopi. How many arms are there?

How many legs are on three rhinos?

How many arms are on two starfish?

How many humps are on one camel?

How many legs do three zebras have?

How many spots are on two ladybugs?

How many rings are on a lemur's tail?

How many pair of antlers are on five stags?

The Arts

Students should know the following animals: the moose, the black bear, the dolphin, the parrot, the ostrich, the alligator, the jaguar, the gila monster, the penguin, the gorilla, the chimpanzee, the elephant, the turtle, the lizard, the fish, the sheep, the lion, the snake, the pig, and the harp seal. Have your students work in teams to make picture cards illustrating these animals.

Two sets of cards can be used together to play a matching game.

Information Literacy

Children are interested in different and possibly bizarre animals. Have them search for pictures of unfamiliar animals at http://www.animalpicturesarchive.com/ or http://www.arkive.org/. Ask them to describe the animals in writing and help make one big list of animals for the classroom.

REFERENCES

Wormell, Christopher. *The New Alphabet of Animals*. Philadelphia: Running Press, 2004.

Learn more about the wood engravings of Christopher Wormell at http://www.theartworksinc.com/face/cwface.htm.

Teeth, Tails, and Tentacles

Across

1. Fine, soft hair covering the bodies of some animals.
5. Flexible outer covering of an animal's body.
7. Between the head and the abdomen of an insect.
9. The covering most birds have on their bodies.
12. Fish use these to push themselves through the water.
13. The part of the body containing the eyes and mouth.
14. Extends behind the animal.
15. The octopus uses this to grab things.
19. Animals walk on two, four, six, or more of these.
20. The last section of an insect body.

Down

1. Part of the whale's tail.
2. Used by bats, flies, and birds to fly.
3. Horny part of a foot.
4. Thin, overlapping plates that protect some animals.
6. Branched, hornlike projections.
7. Helps the starfish move.
8. Used to chew.
10. Used to push through water.
11. A hard outer body covering.
14. The elephant's elongated nose.
16. Elephants and walrus have these.
17. Used to scratch, crush, or climb.
18. A long, projecting nose.

CHAPTER 9

Tree Life: *Meeting Trees*

Written by Scott Russell Sanders

Washington, DC: National Geographic Society, 1997.

SUMMARY

A boy and his father spend a day together in the wood shop and out of doors discovering information about living trees, as well as the uses of fine wood.

RELATED CONCEPTS

Fine wood has specific characteristics by species.

Trees can be identified and appreciated by their shape, leaves, bark, seeds, fruits, and places where they grow.

RELATED VOCABULARY

aspen	redbud
beech	shagbark hickory
black walnut	sweet gum
buckeye	sycamore
maple	tulip tree
mulberry	wild cherry
oak	willow
persimmon	

ACTIVITIES

Language Arts

Janice Urdy wrote a book several years ago called *A Tree Is Nice*, which includes many reasons for the title. Have the students update this children's classic by stating what they think makes a tree "nice." Illustrations should complement the writing.

Select a group of age-appropriate children's literature titles about trees to help students with their research.

Writing

Have each child select a tree from this book or a tree that is indigenous to its area. Describe the tree, where it grows, and its use to animals and humans. Accompany this writing with an illustration of the tree and its leaf, flower, and seed. These can be part of a bulletin board display along with the three art projects described in the arts section.

Social Studies

The United States is divided into climatic zones (see Figure 9.1), which can be used to assist gardeners in selecting plants. Trees too, grow in specific zones. Make a wall chart of well-known trees—for example, the palm tree, and where they grow. Be sure to include ones indigenous to the students' environment.

Wood has many uses, such as in the construction industry. Ask the students to think of other uses for wood, such as making baseball bats and toothpicks. Have display of these items.

Students may wish to select and plant a tree sapling on school property. Consult a nearby nursery or parent volunteer for additional assistance.

Science

To observe the way water and nutrients are transported upward to the leaves and flowers of a plant, take a single stalk of celery. Cut the bottom edge cleanly. Place it in a glass with a little water and food coloring on the bottom. Let the celery sit overnight, upright in the water. The food color can be seen rising in the interior of the celery stalk (see Figure 9.2, p. 54). This is similar to the workings of the tree's transport system.

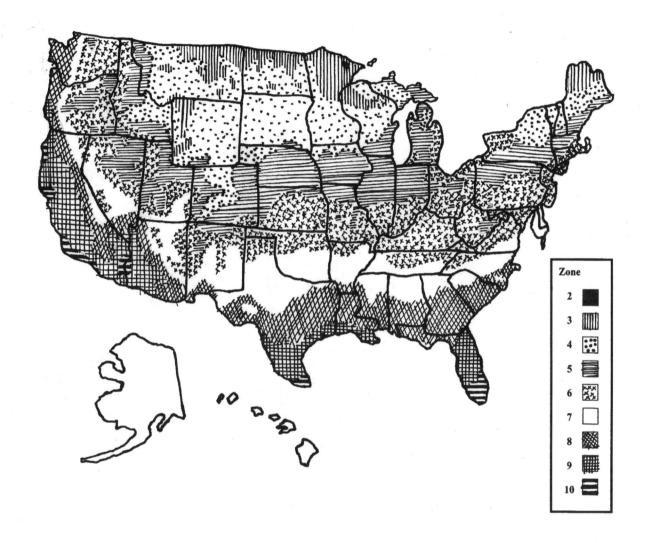

Figure 9.1. U.S. climatic zones

Figure 9.2. Celery circulation

If possible, obtain a short length of unsplit wood from a forest or from a pile of firewood. With hand lenses, discover all the items found in the piece of wood. Categorize them on a table that all can view. Any live critters should be put in a bottle for study and then released a short time later. How does an examination of the tree and its bark help to understand how the tree survives? NOTE: Remember that each ring on the cross section of the tree is equal to a year's growth.

Trees can be recognized at different seasons of the year by a variety of characteristics. To help children learn to identify trees, have them organize a classroom tree museum with sample leaves, nuts, cones, etc., of the common local trees. (See Figure 9.3.) Some characteristics that can help identify trees follow:

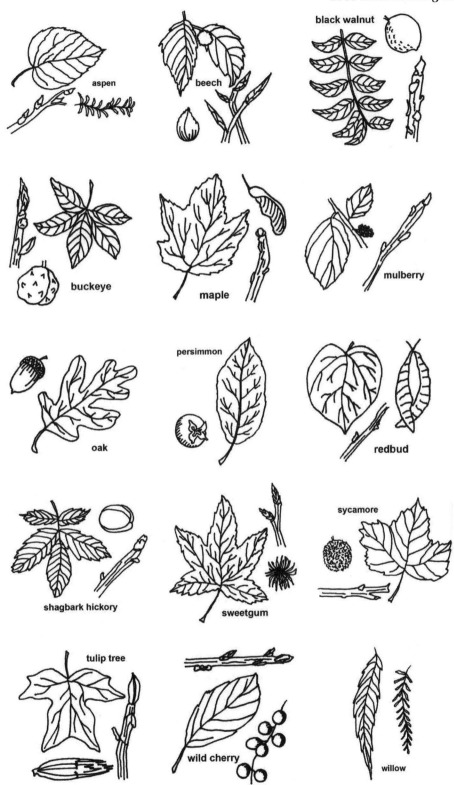

Figure 9.3. Tree identification pictures

Leaves: During the summer and autumn, tree leaves are found on and under trees and may assist in recognition. Very common trees include the red oak, with leaves that have five to eleven triangular lobes pointing upward; birches, with single-pointed ended, egg-shaped leaves; maple, with leaves having three broad lobes; and ash, with leaves that are large and typically made of numerous leaflets, which are elongated and arranged opposite the twig.

Bark: Shagbark hickory trees have bark that curls up in long strips; white birch trees have papery white bark; and sycamore bark appears blotchy and drops off in irregular little plates.

Seeds or nuts: Maple trees have winged seeds; oaks have acorns made of two unequal halves; and many trees produce uniquely shaped nuts or fruits.

Tree shape: Maples often show an overall round shape; willows often are called "weeping," because their arching branches droop to the ground.

Mathematics

Many trees have leaves that are made of parts or leaflets that are composed of a distinctive number of similar parts. White pine trees, for example, have needlelike leaves made up of five needles between three and five inches long. Assemble a collection of tree leaves or drawings that illustrate a differ number of similar parts.

The Arts

Gather several of the falling leaves near the school. Several projects can be made from them.

First, lay a leaf specimen on a piece of clear contact paper that is lying face up. Cut another piece of contact paper and lay in on top of the leaf. The sides can be trimmed to make bookmarks, dream catchers, window hangers, etc. Next, gather a supple leaf that can be flattened between two layers of paper. Holding the paper firmly, rub the flattened side of a crayon over the leaf. The veined side of the leaf should be in contact with the piece of paper covering the leaf. Leaf rubbings then may be trimmed or matted and used for decoration.

Lay a leaf on a paper. With a waxed crayon, cover just the veins in the leaf. Paint the rest of the leaf with water color for a mosaic effect.

Information Literacy

Search the Internet to learn more about the challenges facing forests throughout the world. Associations such as American Forests (http://www.americanforests.org/) encourage the planting of trees in urban as well a rural areas, especially to replace trees lost through natural disasters. Use the American Forests organization and its literature as a basis to learn about how people are helping maintain tree plantings throughout the world.

REFERENCES

The United States Forest Service's Web page provides a link to many materials, including a library of free videos (http://www.fs.fed.us/).

Bergen, Lara Rice. *Looking at Trees and Leaves*. (My First Field Guides). New York: Grosset and Dunlap, 2002.

Cassie, Brian. *Trees*. (National Audubon Society First Field Guide). New York: Scholastic, 1999.

State Departments or Bureaus for Forest Resources often provide valuable educational and information resources. You can find your own state forester through the Web page of the National Association of State Foresters (http://www.stateforesters.org/). For example, the state forester in Pennsylvania provides an online guide to identifying common trees of Pennsylvania at http://www.dcnr.state.pa.us/forestry/commontr/index.aspx.

Meeting Trees

Across

2. Has sweet, pulpy fruit that hangs on the trees after the leaves fall.
5. Has 3 inch tapered leaves and bears seeds in burs.
6. Large heart shaped leaves with seed pods.
10. Three lobed pointed leaves with winged seeds.
12. Small bushy tree with sour red fruit.
13. Bark is smooth and splotchy.
14. Heart shaped leaves and red fruit often eaten by insects.

Down

1. Has warty alligator-like bark and seed balls that fall in winter.
3. Bark is long and stringy.
4. Has acorns as seeds.
5. Large 15 inch leaves with many leaflets, strong beautiful dark brown wood.
7. Four lobed leaves with flattened end.
8. Branches droop, leaves are long and slender.
9. Leaflets arranged like spreading fingers also call "horse chestnut".
11. Has nearly round small "quaking" leaves.

CHAPTER 10

Vegetables and Gardening:
The Ugly Vegetables

Written by Grace Lin
Watertown, MA: Charlesbridge, 1999

SUMMARY

A woman grows Asian vegetables that look strange and unappetizing to her daughter, until she makes soup that delights the neighborhood. Now, everyone wants to grow "ugly vegetables."

RELATED CONCEPTS

Vegetables can be very tasty.

Vegetables can be readily grown in a home garden.

Vegetables develop from germinating seeds to fruiting plants.

RELATED VOCABULARY

broccoli	roots
cabbage	rows
chives	seeds
cucumber	soil
fruits	stems
garden	sunlight
label	vegetables
leaves	water

ACTIVITIES

Language Arts

Have gardening magazines and books available for students to look at and identify various plants. Have each student select a favorite plant and draw a sketch of it for a bulletin board display.

Several days before the unit on gardening begins, place a small, wrapped box on the teacher's desk. The box may be picked up and shaken. Ask the students what is in the box. On the first day of the unit, open the box and take out packages of flower and vegetable seeds. Distribute the packets to small groups or individual students for use as an information source.

Use the back of the seed packet to learn about planting seeds. Categories of information include when the seeds should be planted indoors, how much light they will need, when the seedlings should be transplanted outdoors, what care the plants will need, and when they should be harvested. Elaborate on these stages and review the sequence of events before seeds are planted. NOTE: Inexpensive seed packets can be found at large building supply stores or at stores selling discounted items.

Make a play from the book and have children assume the roles of neighborhood people who learn about the "ugly vegetables." Or use the script at http://www.gracelin.com/media/book/activities_uglyvegscript.pdf.

Writing

Have students bring in recipes for vegetable soup. Write out the list of ingredients as well as the steps in the process of cooking the vegetables. Some students may wish to bring in a can of soup if this is more familiar to them. Show them how to find the ingredient section.

Social Studies

The United States is divided into numbered zones that explain the best conditions under which plants and flowers can grow. Refer to Figure 9.1 for the illustration. Lower-numbered zones are for colder climates; higher-numbered zones are warmer. Compare the information on the seed packets to the zone number in which the students live. Which trees and flowers grow best in the local zone?

Have students locate the zones in which different cities lie. For example, Minneapolis is in zone 4. Miami is in zone 10. What should this tell you about the vegetation in these two cities?

Provide students with blank outline maps of the United States (Figure 10.1) so that they can locate selected cities: New York, NY; Columbia, SC; New Orleans, LA; Columbus, OH; Phoenix, AZ; Fargo, SD; Lexington, KY; Salt Lake City, UT. NOTE: Climatic zones can be added to the outline map.

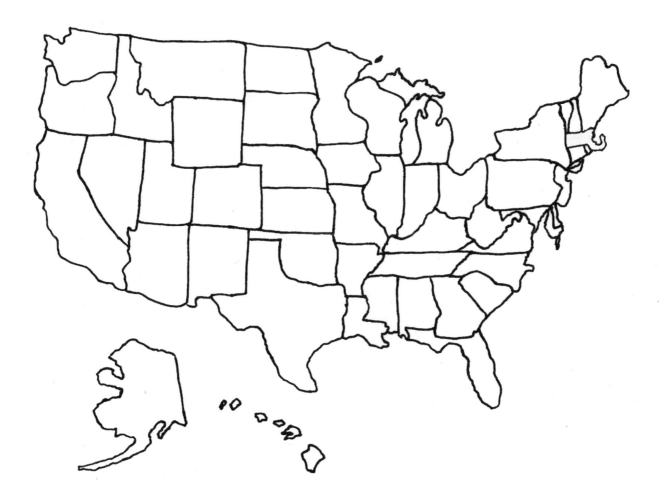

Figure 10.1. U.S. outline map

Science

Examine the outsides and insides of seeds with a hand lens. Notice that there is stored food inside the seed. Is there a difference between flower seeds and vegetable seeds? How will the seeds get nourishment as they grow?

Plant a variety of seeds according to the directions on the packet. You may choose to plant only flowers, only vegetables, or a variety. Check the seed packet to see the number of days it takes to germinate the seeds. When can you expect to have young seedlings? NOTE: Plant seeds in individual cups so that students may take them home for transplanting.

Students should learn that plants will need sunshine, soil, water, and air to thrive. How can students control these variables?

Mathematics

From a list given to the students, take a survey of vegetables that they like or dislike. Chart their answers using a bar graph to discover the most and least favorite vegetables for your students. Students may wish to explain why they do not like certain vegetables. Which veggies are favorites?

Have the students plan a 10-by-10-foot vegetable or flower garden and select the flowers and vegetables they wish to plant. Decide how much area to give each item and how each will be positioned in the garden. Sections of the garden can be marked as fractions or percentages or by laying out certain sized rectangles and squares.

Take a soup recipe and double or triple the amount of ingredients. Also cut the recipe in half.

The Arts

Make identification tags to mark each row of plants as the gardeners in the story did.

Have a "souper" soup day on which parents and students can send in crock pots of soup for lunch. Are any of these ethnic soups, like Mexican chili?

Information Literacy

Ask groups of three or four students each to research which Asian vegetables they would want to grow. There are several online suppliers of seeds, such as http://www.agrohaitai. com/onlinecatelogue.htm, to consult.

REFERENCES

Dooley, Nora. *Everybody Cooks Rice*. New York: Scholastic Press, 1992

Rattigan, Jama Kim. *Dumpling Soup*. New York: Little, Brown, 1993.

Sanmugam, Devagi. *Fun with Asian Food: A Kid's Cookbook*. North Clarendon, VT: Tuttle Publishing, 2005.

Wells, Rosemary. *Yoko*. New York: Hyperion Books, 1998.

The Ugly Vegetables

Across

3. A variety of cauliflower with green leaves and small flowers.
5. The flat parts of the plant that grow from branches on the stem.
7. The energy source for plant growth.
9. The liquid that helps plants grow.
11. A green or purple vegetable forming a head.
12. A place to grow plants.
13. The loose part of the ground where plants grow.
14. Formed in the fruit of the plant and capable of growing into new plants.
15. A small, onion-flavored plant.

Down

1. The fleshy part of the plant that bears the seeds.
2. Straight lines of plants growing in the garden.
4. A long, green fruit eaten in salads or pickled.
6. Parts of plants that humans eat.
8. Placing the name on the plant's place in the garden.
10. The underground part of the plant.
13. The longest part of the plant, joining the roots with the leaves and fruit.

Part 2

The Earth, the Atmosphere, and the Universe

CHAPTER 11

Invention of the Airplane:
My Brothers' Flying Machine

Written by Jane Yolen
New York: Little, Brown, 2003

SUMMARY

Katharine, the sister of the Wright brothers, tells the story of her family and how her brothers researched and built the first airplane to fly.

RELATED CONCEPTS

Katharine Wright helped her brothers manage their business.

The Wright brothers built their first airplane after years of research on kites and gliders.

The Wright brothers determined the best shape for wings using a wind tunnel.

The Wright brothers were successful bicycle makers before building aircraft.

RELATED VOCABULARY

Chanute	flying machine
Charlie Taylor	glider
Dayton	Kitty Hawk
engine	rubber band motor
fabric	Smithsonian
flyer	wood

ACTIVITIES

Language Arts

Both of the Wright brothers agreed that their sister helped them tremendously in their work. How was this possible when she was not part of their experiments and did not fly for many years after the airplane had been invented? Ask students to work in small groups using the graphic organizer shown in Figure 11.1 to organize the ways they see this influence on the outcome of the story.

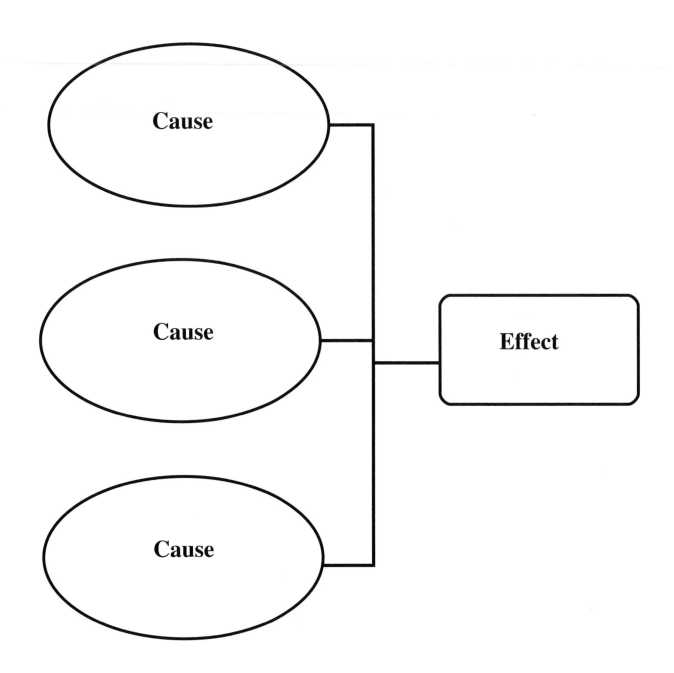

Figure 11.1 Wright Brothers graphic organizer

Writing

"The best thing about flying is _____" or "The best part of flying would be _____" are exciting journal entries.

Learn about other pioneers of aviation in the early twentieth century—for example, Louis Bleriot, Charles Lindbergh, Glenn Curtis, Bessie Coleman, Jacqueline Cochran, Amelia Earhart, Chuck Yeager, and Sally Ride. Obtain additional names from the Internet and combine them on a timeline of twentieth-century aviation.

Make an acrostic in which each letter of a specific word is replaced by a word or phrase about the item. For example:

A   cceleration

I   n the air

R   acing forward

P   owered flight

L   anding gently

A   eroplane

N   ever gave up

E   xperimenters

Social Studies

On the map of the United States in Figure 10.1, locate the Wright brothers' home in Dayton, Ohio and their experimentation locations in Kill Devil Hills and Kitty Hawk, North Carolina.

Visit a local airport and observe its operation. Can someone provide an explanation on how a plane takes off and lands? If a student trip cannot be arranged, a guest speaker or video might be very informative.

Science

As a class project, help the children work in groups to test wing designs in a classroom wind tunnel. The Wright brothers made their tunnel out of a large cardboard box with a window in the side and a powered fan to provide a constant source of air. Cut a hole in one end of a box approximately two cubic feet in size and provide a hole in the front for the air to escape. Anchor test wings in the middle of the box with a string tightly holding each end. An electric fan with a good safety cage on it can be used to power the wind tunnel. A responsible adult must be present to supervise the use of the fan to ensure that fingers and other objects do not come into contact with the fan blades. The lift of the wing can be measured with a spring balance. This is how the Wright brothers measured lift in their wind tunnel.

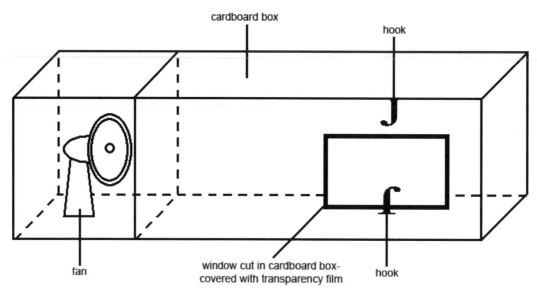

Figure 11.2 Wind tunnel diagram

The last decade of the nineteenth century and the first decade of the twentieth saw a great deal of experimentation and interest in the possibility and reality of powered human flight. Assist the class in learning more about the other aviation pioneers who worked at the same time as the Wright brothers. Some other early pioneers were Otto Lilienthal, Samuel Pierpont Langley, Octave Chanute, Glenn Curtiss, and Louis Bleriot.

Mathematics

Have students guess the answers to the following:

What was the weight of the *Flyer*?

How far did it travel?

How long did the first flight last?

How high did the plane fly?

The answers are:

The weight of twenty-six full-sized bicycles, about 605 pounds.

The length of 2½ school busses, about 120 feet.

As long as you can hold your breath, about twelve seconds.

The height of a basketball hoop, ten to fifteen feet.

The Arts

The first airplane to fly successfully was called the *Flyer* by its builders well before it flew in December 1903. The *Flyer* is now on display in the Smithsonian Institution in Washington, D.C. Have the children gain an understanding of the *Flyer* by coloring the sketch of the airplane (Figure 11.3).

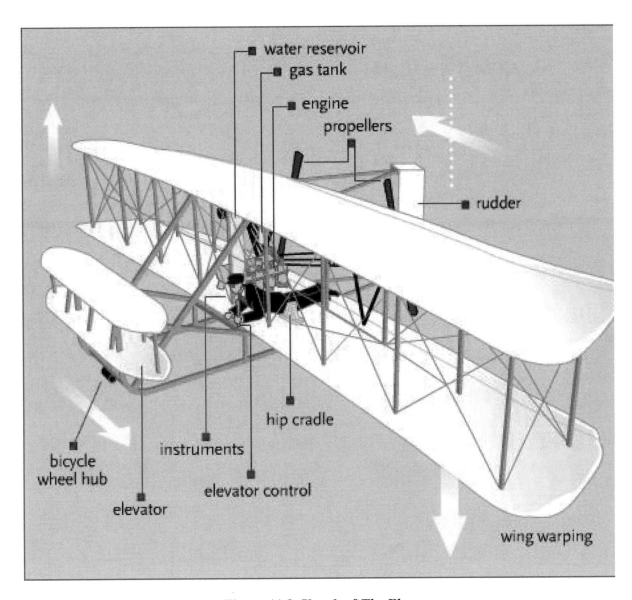

Figure 11.3. Sketch of *The Flyer*

From *The Natural World Through Children's Literature: An Integrated Approach* by Carol M. Butzow and John W. Butzow. Westport, CT: Libraries Unlimited/Teacher Ideas Press. Copyright © 2007.

Information Literacy

There is a great deal of supporting information on the Internet about the Wright brothers and their *Flyer*. Challenge the class to produce a picture gallery of photos, drawings, and related materials or a timeline.

REFERENCES

Butzow, Carol M., and John W. Butzow. *Science Through Children's Literature.*, 2d ed. Englewood, CO: Libraries Unlimited, 2000. Chapter 33 provides activities related to flight and aircraft, featuring the Provensens' book on Louis Bleriot.

Howard, Fred. *Wilber and Orville: A Biography of the Wright Brothers*. Mineola, NY: Dover Publications, 1998. A good, up-to-date reference for adults on the Wright brothers.

Provensen, Alice, and Martin Provensen. *The Glorious Flight*. New York: Viking Penguin, 1983. A picture book describing the first flight across the English Channel by Louis Bleriot.

INTERNET RESOURCES

http://www.nasm.si.edu/wrightbrothers/. A detailed Web page developed by the National Air and Space Museum of the Smithsonian Institution in honor of the 100th anniversary of the Wright brothers' first flight.

http://www.nps.gov/wrbr/. The Web page of the National Park Service's Visitor's Center near Kitty Hawk, North Carolina.

My Brothers' Flying Machine

Across

1. The name the Wright brothers gave their first airplane.
3. Made the first airplane engine for the Wright brothers.
5. Hometown in Ohio of the Wright brothers.
7. Powered many airplane models before humans flew.
10. The largest U.S. museum, in Washington, D.C.

Down

1. Powered aircraft.
2. Its flight is powered only by the wind.
3. French-American engineer who encouraged the Wright brothers.
4. Covered the first airplane.
6. The North Carolina site where the first flight took place.
8. Needed for powered flight.
9. Formed the structure of the first airplanes.

From *The Natural World Through Children's Literature: An Integrated Approach* by Carol M. Butzow and John W. Butzow. Westport, CT: Libraries Unlimited/Teacher Ideas Press. Copyright © 2007.

CHAPTER 12

Discovery of an Ichthyosaur: *Fossil Girl*

Written by Catherine Brighton
London: Frances Lincoln, 2000

SUMMARY

As a girl, Mary Anning found and collected rare fossils to help her family financially. She became one of the first persons to work with fossils professionally.

RELATED CONCEPTS

Mary Anning was among the very first fossil experts, or paleontologists.

Paleontologists are scientists specializing in the study of fossils and the ancient environments in which these living things existed.

Ancient seas were the homes of fishlike reptiles, including ichthyosaurs and plesiosaurs, and birdlike reptiles called pterodactyls.

RELATED VOCABULARY

ammonite	paleontologist
curiosity	plesiosaur
fossil	pterodactyl
ichthyosaur	reptile

ACTIVITIES

Language Arts

Use the graphic organizer given in Figure 12.1 to list four events from the story. What conclusion can be drawn from this information?

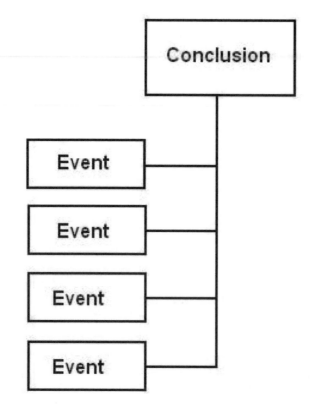

Figure 12.1. *Fossil Girl* **graphic organizer**

Why do students think that the author made this story in the genre of a comic book? Did this appeal to students? Can they create additional scenes of Mary's life? Can they make a comic book for another scientific discovery?

Writing

Write a journal page about the discovery of the ichthyosaur. Do this from the point of view of Mary or her brother, Joseph.

Mary Anning is still an excellent role model for girls around the world. Explain how her life could influence young ladies then and now.

Why were people eager to buy Mary's curiosities? Why were they interested in the discovery of the ichthyosaur? Why are people today still fascinated by fossils?

Was Mary a paleontologist? She was not trained at the university but was self-taught and knew much about this period in history. Does this make her a paleontologist?

Social Studies

On a map of Europe, locate the country of England and the city of Lyme Regis. At the time of this story, what form of transportation would have been used to get from the United States to England? What forms of transportation would have been used within the country?

Figure 12.2. Map of Lyme Regis

Describe the cliffs along the Lyme Regis coast. What kind of rock made up these cliffs? How was the rock washed away and the fossils exposed? Why were they called curiosities?

Make a timeline of the nineteenth century when Mary lived in Lyme Regis. Include events in England, the United States, and around the world. NOTE: *The World Almanac* is an excellent source of information.

Science

Examine real fossils or plastic replicas. What can be seen in the fossil? Is this an entire animal or plant or merely a portion of one? Make a drawing of a fossil animal or plant. How old is the fossil? What time period does the fossil or replica represent?

Make a fossil using plaster of paris. Coat the item, such as a sea shell, with a light but thorough coating of spray cooking oil to ensure it can be removed from the casting process. Place the item on a sheet of aluminum foil. Fold the foil around the item to make a container. Mix the plaster of paris according to the instructions and pour it into the aluminum foil container. Once the plaster of paris has hardened, usually after a day, remove the original item and the aluminum foil carefully from the cast of the item. This is one kind of "fossil," made as a negative of the original. You can repeat the process with the cast as the new item in the aluminum foil container. Use more plaster of paris to make a new positive, three-dimensional copy of the original.

How did Mary know that a storm was coming? What are additional predictors of the weather—for example, "Red sky at night, sailors' delight; red sky at morning, sailors take warning." NOTE: The Internet is an excellent source of these sayings.

Cover a small plastic toy in a mound of sand inside a large container. Slowly push the water up to the sand as the tide would. What eventually happens? What word explains this action? How does this relate to the uncovering of Mary's curiosities? (See Figure 12.3.)

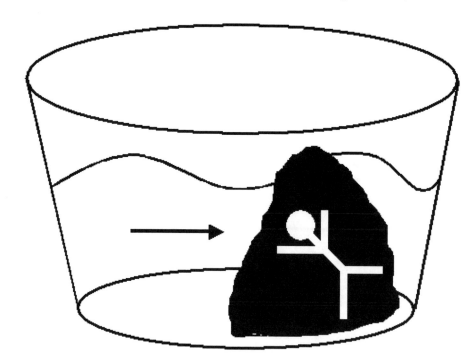

Figure 12.3. Tidal beach activity

Ammonites were the most common of Mary's curiosities (see Figure 12.4). View them on the Internet or purchase samples from Ward's Scientific Inc., in Rochester, New York.

Figure 12.4. Ammonite

Many fossils are found at the top of a mountain or as part of an outcropping. How do sea-like fossils come to be found at mountaintops?

Obtain several curiosities and decide what the animal was. Draw a picture of the animal. Make inferences about how the animal moved and ate. How does this increase the students' understanding of the appearance and movements of ancient marine reptiles?

Use the Internet to research additional information about the ichthyosaur, plesiosaur, and other seagoing dinosaurs that lived in this same geological time period.

Mathematics

The fossils that Mary Anning found at Lyme Regis were very old. They are dated from the Jurassic Era, 200 Ma (million years ago) to about 146 Ma. Practice writing numbers leading up to one million and beyond. Help children conceptualize large numbers by making models that contain large numbers of items, such as a cubic meter of space, which contains one million cubic centimeters, (This would be the space under the typical teacher's desk.) How many million cubic centimeters are there in the classroom?

The Arts

Make finger puppets of well-known dinosaurs. Use felt for the body and notions such as rickrack for the ornamentation of marine reptiles. These can be placed together on the bulletin board for a celebration of "Mary Anning Day."

Information Literacy

Learn more about Mary Anning. Start with the museum Web site http://www. lymeregismuseum.co.uk/, from Mary's home town of Lyme Regis in southern England.

REFERENCES

Books for Children

Atkins, Jeannine. *Mary Anning and the Sea Dragon*. New York: Farrar, Straus & Giroux, 1999.

Brown, Don. *Rare Treasure: Mary Anning and Her Remarkable Discoveries*. New York: Houghton Mifflin, 1999.

Cole, Sheila. *The Dragon in the Cliff: A Novel Based on the Life of Mary Anning*. New York: Lothrop Lee & Shepard, 1991.

Rhodes, Frank H. T. *Fossils*. New York: Golden Guides from St. Martin's Press, 2001.

Books for Adults

Goodhue, Thomas W. *Curious Bones: Mary Anning and the Birth of Paleontology*. Greensboro, NC: Morgan Reynolds Publishing, 2002.

Fossil Girl

Across

2. Mary Anning called her fossils _____.
5. An extinct flying reptile.
6. She found rare fossils while still a child.
8. A marine reptile with a long neck.

Down

1. Remains of living things preserved in rock.
3. A dolphin-like marine reptile.
4. The class of animals that includes turtles, snakes, and alligators.
7. A squid-like shellfish that is found fossilized along with ichthyosaurs

CHAPTER 13

Landforms and Bodies of Water:
M Is for Majestic

Written by David Domeniconi

Chelsea, MI: Sleeping Bear Press, 2003

SUMMARY

Landforms of America are portrayed in this alphabet book about the National Park System.

RELATED CONCEPTS

The National Park System was created to preserve important scenery, natural and historic objects, as well as wildlife, and leave them unspoiled for the enjoyment of future generations.

The National Park System promotes conservation—wise use—of beautiful and rare national places.

The National Park System also preserves certain places and restricts use of them to ensure that their value to the nation remains unchanged.

The National Park System encompasses a wide variety of environments including lakes, seashores, wetlands, mountains, prairies, forests, rivers, canyons, deserts, islands, and glaciers.

RELATED VOCABULARY

badland	island
canyon	mesa
cavern	mountain
crater	petrified Forest
desert	plateau
everglades	prairie
fjord	river
geyser	seashore
glacier	volcano

ACTIVITIES

Language Arts

Students can increase their vocabulary with other national park superlatives—for example, A is for awesome, B is for beautiful, etc. A thesaurus can be of help.

The book *America the Beautiful* gives additional visions of the United States.

Theodore Roosevelt and John Muir were both instrumental in starting the National Park System. Find out more about these farsighted men.

Writing

National parks are becoming overcrowded. Some parks wish to exclude automobiles from the park in favor of less-polluting, high-occupancy vehicles such as busses. Write your opinion on this controversy—should cars continue to be allowed into the parks, or should tourists be required to ride on transportation provided by the park?

Why do we have national parks? What place do they hold in our society? Have the students pick a national park and write why they would like to visit this place.

NOTE: Have other books about national parks available for research.

Social Studies

National parks are created in areas of low or nonexistent population. What is it that attracts tourists but not permanent settlers?

Some preserved lands are home to Native American drawings called petroglyphs. Check the Web sites in the references to learn about them. Have the students try to replicate these pictures.

Science

Our national parks are a study in landforms. Be sure each student can identify a mountain, hill, plateau, mesa, seashore, river valley, canyon, and cave. Find examples of each and name their state—for example, the Grand Canyon in Arizona. Put colored push pins in a map to indicate the location of different landforms.

Invent a national park. Select the state in which it will be located. Indicate the landforms and climate to be found there. Give names to the park itself, natural wonders, rivers, and nearby cities and identify transportation availability. Write a short history of the park and describe its outstanding features—for example, waterfalls, fossil outcrops, vegetation, and animals.

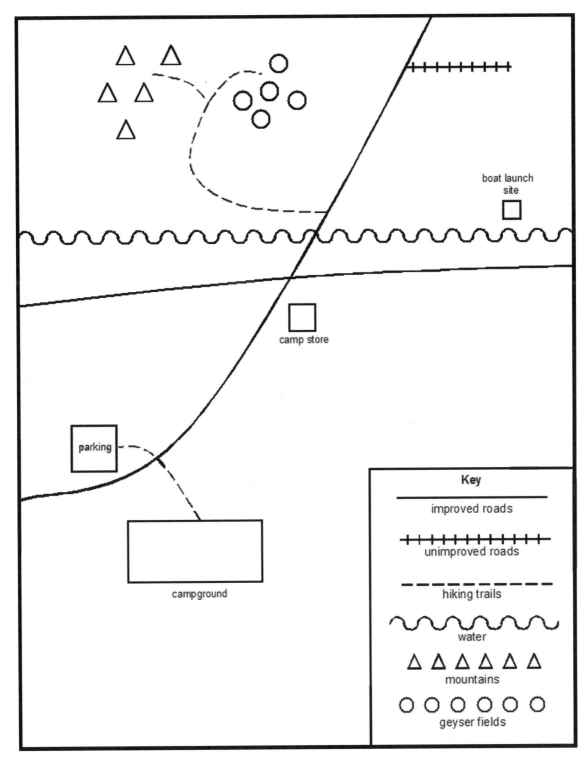

boat launch
site

camp store

parking

campground

Key

improved roads

+++++++++++++ unimproved roads

- - - - - hiking trails

water

△ △ △ △ △
mountains

○ ○ ○ ○ ○ ○
geyser fields

Figure 13.1 Create a park

Mathematics

The area of a national park is measured in acres. An acre is about the size of two football fields. Select the ten largest parks and rank order their acreage. These may also be graphed. Make up questions about the parks—for example, which is the largest? Which are west of the Mississippi River, etc?

Are the largest parks necessarily the most popular or most visited? Compare these two lists. What do the most visited parks have to offer to attract vacationers?

How many parks does each state have? Many states have no national parks. Many do have parks, and these can be graphed—for example, Maine has one national park, Virginia has one, Arizona has three, etc. Use a bar graph for each state.

The Arts

Listen to the *Grand Canyon Suite* by Ferde Grofe. What pictures does this piece bring to mind? You can learn more about this famous composer from the web site http://www.sbgmusic. com/html/teacher/reference/composers/grofe.html.

Draw a map of the national park you created. Include a visitor center; major and minor transportation routes; bicycle, hiking, and nature trails; campgrounds; visitor attractions; nature preserves; mountains; and rivers, streams, and lakes. NOTE: Be sure that all attractions can be reached by some form of transportation.

Design a commemorative stamp that shows an outstanding feature of your park.

Information Literacy

Ask the class to develop a list of issues related to keeping up the National Park System. The National Parks Conservation Association (http://www.npca.org) is a source of information about issues related to the U.S. National Parks. Visit the National Park Service Web site (http://www.nps.gov) or the National Geographic Society Web site for teachers and children (http://www.nationalgeographic.com/education/).

REFERENCES

Bates, Katharine Lee. *America the Beautiful.* New York: Aladdin Paperbacks, 1993.

Locker, Thomas. *John Muir: America's Naturalist.* Golden, CO: Fulcrum Publishing, 2003.
A wonderful children's book about the first public advocate for National Parks.

Murphy, Frank. *The Legend of the Teddy Bear.* Chelsea, MI: Sleeping Bear Press, 2000.

Pictures of Native American rock art or petroglyphs can be found at: http://www.musnaz. org/exhibits/images/SOS_Web125.jpg and www.spiritcanyon.com.

M Is for Majestic

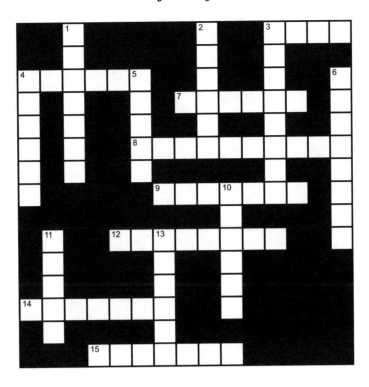

Across

3. High rocky plateau with very steep sides.
4. A large bowl-shaped hole possibly made by a huge object hitting the earth.
7. Land completely surrounded by water.
8. A huge wetland in South Florida.
9. A large hill where hot gasses, molten rock, and cinders come out of the earth.
12. Eroded hills in the Dakotas.
14. A large flat, wild grassland.
15. An area of very high level ground.

Down

1. A river of ice.
2. Steam, hot water, and mud blown from the earth.
3. A very high hill.
4. A cave or very huge underground hollow place.
5. A large stream.
6. Where the ocean and land meet.
10. Rock cut by a river; the most famous is in Arizona
11. Long narrow inlet of the sea.
13. A very dry part of the country; we have a painted one.

From *The Natural World Through Children's Literature: An Integrated Approach* by Carol M. Butzow and John W. Butzow. Westport, CT: Libraries Unlimited/Teacher Ideas Press. Copyright © 2007.

CHAPTER 14

Water Conservation:
The Incredible Water Show

Written by Debra Frasier
New York: Harcourt, 2004

SUMMARY

A neighborhood performance teaches parents and children the importance of water.

RELATED CONCEPTS

The water cycle traces water from evaporation through precipitation to its return to the ocean and around again.

Water is scarce in many parts of the world and needs to be conserved.

Water purity is a big problem that the whole world faces.

Potable water, or water pure enough to drink, is necessary to life and is very valuable.

RELATED VOCABULARY

clouds	potable
condense	precipitation
conserve	rivers
cycle	sleet
earth	snow
evaporate	springs
hydrogen	storm
land	stream
molecule	vapor
ocean	water
oxygen	

ACTIVITIES

Language Arts

Produce a water show similar to the one in the book. In this presentation about water, indicate its source, how is it used, how and why must it be conserved, and how the earth continuously maintains its water levels.

Writing

Water Dance by Thomas Locker is a highly visual book that illustrates the water cycle.

Write the story of a raindrop and how it spends its day. Be sure that the processes of the water cycle are contained in the story.

Social Studies

Seventy-five percent of the globe is covered by water. On the world map provided in Figure 1.2, locate the oceans and seas that are part of this vast body of water. Which oceans or seas touch the United States?

Have the children prepare a definition of the word "drought." A detailed presentation is found at http://www.drought.unl.edu/kids/whatis.htm.

A drought is a drop in rainfall from that which is normally expected. Read *The Water Hole* by Graeme Base to see the effects of a drought on the animal population.

Locate the areas on the earth that are continuously plagued by drought. See, for example, http://www.das.uwyo.edu/~geerts/cwx/notes/chap10/drought.html. What are the effects of this condition?

NOTE: Also see activities in chapter 20 for *The Water Hole* by Graeme Base.

Science

Water is continuously evaporating and condensing in the atmosphere. This is called the water cycle. As rain falls, it becomes runoff from the earth, or flows into streams and rivers that lead to the ocean. Water vapor evaporates from the ocean and rises to meet cooler air in the clouds. The water condenses out of the cloud and falls to the earth as rain.

Students can demonstrate their understanding of the water cycle through drawings, pantomimes, spoken presentations, or by sequencing cards that indicate each step of the water cycle. (See Figure 14.1.)

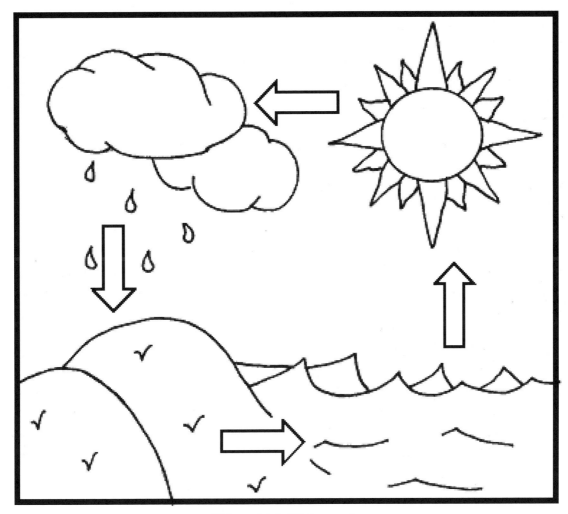

Figure 14.1. Water cycle

Place a jar of water on the windowsill and mark the water level. Each day, check the level of the water to see how much has evaporated. Students may wish to calculate how much is gone each day by measuring the exact amount of water left. (See Figure 14.2.)

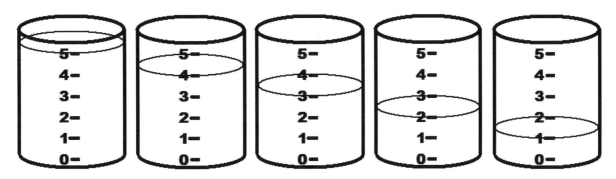

Figure 14.2. Water levels in beakers

Place a glass full of ice cubes on the table. Observe how the water vapor in the air condenses onto the outside of the glass. Explain this. Does the temperature of the room affect the rate at which this happens?

Place a plastic bottle of water in the freezer. What happens when the water expands? Link this reaction to the weathering of rocks, the cracking of highways, and the breaking of sidewalks.

Mathematics

What is the annual precipitation level in the state or community where the students live? Is theirs a dry, average, or wet climate? Compare this to other cities or states. NOTE: *The World Almanac* is an excellent source for this information.

The Arts

Students may make posters or placards bearing facts about water to carry as part of their presentation of the story of water. Placards might indicate that 75 percent of the earth is covered by water, the human body is 60 percent water, the water we use has been around since the days of the dinosaurs, etc.

Design posters or bumper stickers advocating the conservation of water.

Display copies of paintings that are indicative of water. You may refer to artists such as Winslow Homer.

Calendars often show oceans, lakes, waterfalls, seashores, lighthouses, etc. Discuss how the water that is shown is part of the water cycle and how it is important to people on the earth.

Partake in an instructional unit on the use of watercolor. How is this technique different from other forms of painting?

Information Literacy

Have the children work in groups to use the Internet to describe many ways of conserving fresh water. See http://www.h2ouse.org/tour/index.cfm for suggestions for saving water around the house.

REFERENCES

Base, Graeme. *The Water Hole.* New York: Puffin Books, 2001.

Locker, Thomas. *Water Dance.* San Diego: Harcourt Brace, 1997.

http://www.americanwater.com/49ways.htm. A Web site suggesting forty-nine ways to save water.

http://www.wateruseitwisely.com/. A Web site that provides a checklist on wise water use.

The Incredible Water Show
EVAPORATION

Across

3. Three-fourths of the _____ is covered with water.
6. Water that is safe to drink.
7. They flow to the ocean.
10. Rainwater runs off the _____ to a body of water.
11. Water that falls from the sky.

Down

1. Rain, snow, and sleet are forms of _____.
2. Smaller than a river.
4. Smallest particle of water.
5. This cycle assures us that we will have water.
8. When water becomes invisible, it is called _____.
9. Can be the source of a river.

The Incredible Water Show
CONDENSATION

Across

1. Vapor condenses out of the _____.
4. The lightest element.
7. Going in a circle.
10. Water _____ into the air.
12. To form droplets of water.

Down

2. Combined with hydrogen in water.
3. Falling crystals of ice.
5. To move upward.
6. A mixture of rain and snow.
8. The largest body of water.
9. To save or use wisely
11. Violent conditions in the sky.

CHAPTER 15

Meteorites: *Call Me Ahnighito*

Written by Pam Conrad
New York: HarperCollins, 1995

SUMMARY

Written in the first person, this is the story of a meteorite that eventually comes to live in New York City.

RELATED CONCEPTS

Meteorites are rocks that fall to earth from elsewhere in the solar system.

Most meteorites are made primarily of iron.

Meteorites can produce large craters when they fall to earth or they can be miniscule in size.

RELATED VOCABULARY

axes	hydraulic jacks
barge	ice floe
blizzard	picks
crane	procession
gangplanks	tides
hammering	tugboats
hold (of ship)	winches

ACTIVITIES

Language Arts

Use a KWL graphic organizer for this unit. Fold a paper into three vertical columns entitled K—What I know about the topic, W—What I want to learn about the topic, and L—What I learned from the lesson. Compare students' findings.

What is a meteorite? Where do they come from? What are they made from? How do they affect the earth?

Make an acrostic about meteorites. For example:

M	ost burn up
E	arth receives thousands each year
T	hey come from asteroids
E	xtremely rare
O	rigins in outer space
R	ocklike
I	t forms a crater
T	hey fall from the sky
E	arly man believed they were from the gods

This story is written in the first person—that is, the story is told by the main character. All of the events of the story happened to that character. Do the students prefer this method of writing, or the more common third person? Have the students write a short story in the first person.

Writing

It was very expensive and time consuming to transport the meteorite to New York City. Is this a wanton waste of money and resources, or is this balanced out by the enjoyment and information people will get from observing and studying the meteorite? Take a position and support your decision in a short essay.

It is the day of the dedication of the meteorite at the American Museum of Natural History. Write a tribute to Ahnighito in the form of a poem, an anecdote, a song, a newspaper story, a choral reading, etc. This writing may include Ahnighito's past history as well as the events taking place in New York City in 1893.

Social Studies

Locate Ahnighito's first home on earth, Greenland, and New York City, where it now resides. What problems were encountered moving the meteorite from Greenland to New York City? Why was it called Ahnighito?

The museum dedication took place in 1893. How do the illustrations in the book depict that time in U.S. history?

The American Museum of Natural History is world famous. Using the museum Web site, find out about other items on display. Where is the museum located? When is it open? How much is the admission price?

Ask students to discuss why there are museums. What is their purpose? Why do individuals and groups of persons visit museum displays? Would it not be less expensive and more time worthy to read articles about the objects? Take a poll of the students to see which side of this issue they would support. Would students want to visit a museum that is available to the community?

Science

In the story, much is made of the condition in Greenland called the Arctic winter. Discuss the fact that the length of the day grows shorter as December nears. Contrary to that, the length of the days grows longer as June approaches. How does this situation impact the lives of the students in those areas when winter days equal twenty-four hours of darkness and summer days equal twenty-four hours of daylight?

Meteorites are made of rock with very high iron content. How did this affect the compass on the ship carrying Ahnighito? Of what use are rocks with high iron content?

Mathematics

How far was it from Ahnighito's original home in Greenland to its home in New York City? Use a globe for more accurate measurement than a flat projection map.

Measure out the size of Ahnighito in a large room or hallway. The metric measurements are 3.2 X 2.1 X 1.7 meters. It weighs thirty-four tons—this is about the weight of two school busses or ten autos.

The Cape York meteorites consist of Ahnighito, the Woman, and the Dog. See if you can find the size of these two smaller pieces. NOTE: They are in the same museum as Ahnighito.

The Arts

The key words "Inuit tools-meteorite" will open up several Internet sites showing Inuit tools made from meteorites. Other Inuit artifacts are found under the key words "Inuit art."

What information do you find about Inuit art on the Internet?

Information Literacy

Excellent information on meteorites can be obtained from the Web site htw.amnh.org/exhibitions/permanent/meteorites/what.

REFERENCES

http://www.amnh.org/exhibitions/permanent/meteorites/what/ahnighito.php. A Web site from the American Museum of Natural History describing Ahnighito's exhibit.

http://cfa-www.harvard.edu/cfa/ps/icq/meteorites.html. A Web site at the Harvard-Smithsonian Center for Astrophysics listing meteorites that fell to earth during the past 200 years.

Call Me Ahnighito

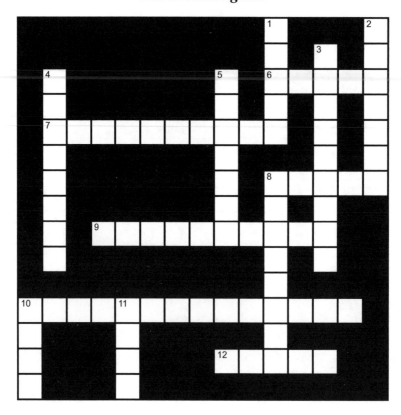

Across

6. A machine used to lift heavy objects.
7. Walkways used to load ships.
8. A flat-bottomed boat towed by a powered boat to haul freight.
9. A slow, solemn march to escort an important person or object.
10. Powerful jacks that use pressure to move objects.
12. The daily changes in water level along the sea coast.

Down

1. Tools used to crack ice.
2. A huge moving sheet of ocean ice.
3. The sound made by repeated blows of a hammer.
4. Powerful boats used to tow or push ships.
5. Machines used to pull in ropes or chains attached to anchors or other heavy objects.
8. A blinding snowstorm.
10. The lowest deck of a ship used for stowing freight.
11. Large hatchets used to chop wood and ice.

CHAPTER 16

Discovery of a Comet: *Maria's Comet*

Written by Deborah Hopkinson
New York: Aladdin Paperbacks, 1999

SUMMARY

Maria Mitchell's father encouraged her interest in the stars as she was growing up in nineteenth-century Nantucket. Her later discovery of a comet led to her designation as the first American woman astronomer.

RELATED CONCEPTS

Most heavenly bodies travel in space following fixed patterns.

The visible universe is made up of stars, planets, moons, asteroids, dust clouds, gas, comets, and nebulae.

Many comets orbit the sun in elliptical orbits taking many years to complete.

Astronomers systematically study the makeup and motion of heavenly bodies.

RELATED VOCABULARY

asteroid	moon
astronomer	planet
comet	Polaris
constellation	star
Copernicus	telescope
explorer	whaling
Galileo	

ACTIVITIES

Language Arts

Maria had many chores around the house, like caring for her brothers and sisters or helping them with their lessons. Still, she and her father arranged to have time together for her lessons. Take a survey of what chores children have to do in the afternoon and evening. Do they make time to sit with another family member and work together or study? What changes could be made to make more time?

Ask the students to use the Venn diagram in Figure 16.1 to compare Maria Mitchell's life with that of Mary Anning, whose life is described in chapter 12. Suggest that they consider comparing when they lived, where they lived, their accomplishments in the world of science, and the level of fame they each achieved.

Mary   Maria

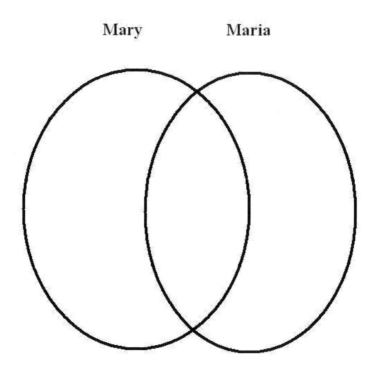

Figure 16.1. Venn diagram: Mary—Maria

What kind of teacher was Mr. Mitchell? What kind of student was Maria? How did they work so well together? Assign working partners in the classroom and designate a topic for them to research.

Writing

Have the students decide what they would like to discover or accomplish in their lifetimes. This need not be a discovery in space, but could be any topic of their choosing. Have them write a story telling how this discovery happens.

Social Studies

Locate Nantucket Island off the coast of Massachusetts (see Figure 16.2). The Mitchell family lived here. Maria also lived near Poughkeepsie, New York, when she taught at Vassar. Locate this college.

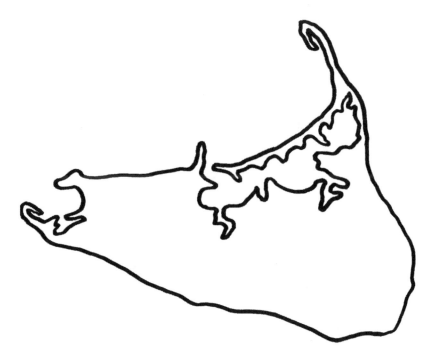

Figure 16.2. Map of Nantucket

Maria Mitchell's childhood home has become a museum. There is information about the house and museum activities on the Web at http://www.mmo.org/index.php.

Discuss what advantages an area must have to be a good harbor. Look at the map of Nantucket and mark those places that might make a good harbor. Check to see if you have chosen well. Why was Nantucket the most famous whaling town in the world?

Whaling was a very profitable occupation for men from Nantucket, including Maria's own brother. Whale oil was essential to the lighting of lamps for illumination. Learn more about whaling from these sources: The Nantucket Historical Association's Whaling Museum's Web site at http://www.nha.org/exhibits/index.html; and The New Bedford Whaling Museum, which provides a great deal of information online at http://www.whalingmuseum.org/kendall/index_KI.html.

Science

Science involves painstaking and detailed observation of phenomena. Often there may seem to be little change to report, but even the most minute change may be very significant. To help students increase their powers of observation, ask them to make observations of a specific part of the night sky every day for two weeks. Provide opportunities to talk abut the observations daily. Encourage drawing, videotaping, or digital photography to supplement what can be remembered by the naked eyes alone. Have students keep a journal in which they draw and describe the changes that they observe. They should learn to use clear, concise language and to make inferences about what will happen next.

NOTE: Observation of the night sky requires parental supervision to ensure the safety of the children involved. This is a great activity to involve the whole family and invite families to come to the school to share their experiences.

Mathematics

Whalers used many instruments for fixing their position and direction as they sailed as far as the Pacific Ocean. These instruments included highly accurate watches called chronometers (see Figure 16.3; for another picture, see http://www.manitobamuseum.mb.ca/sg_marine.html).

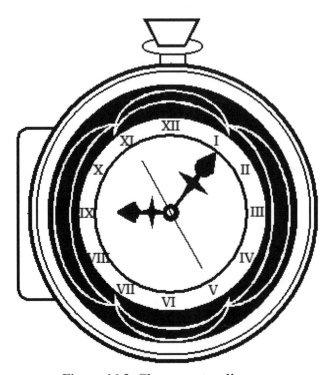

Figure 16.3. Chronometer diagram

One of Mr. Mitchell's jobs was to adjust these pieces for the sea captains. When he was away on business, Maria would often perform this service. To find the distance between two places on the earth, you need to know the precise time at each location. If the home location time is 12:00 midnight and the local time is precisely 12:00 noon, it is half the circumference (24,902 miles or 40,076 km at the equator) of the earth from home to the current location. Make up examples like this for distances equivalent to time differences of 6:00 A.M. and noon and 10:00 A.M. and noon.

Mathematics is very important to astronomers. Some of the mathematics that is important to the study of comets is based on the ellipse, the shape of the orbit of many comets. Children can make an ellipse with a pencil, a loop of string, a board, and two thumbtacks. Follow the diagram (Figure 16.4) to see how the pencil is always kept equidistant from both of the two foci of the ellipse.

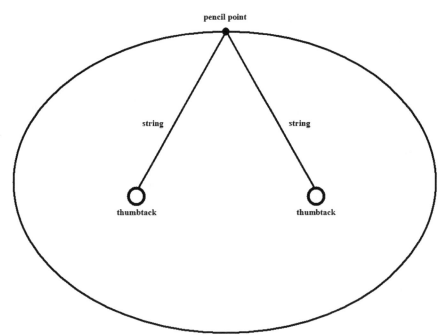

Figure 16.4. Drawing an ellipse

The Arts

In later life, Maria Mitchell was the first person to see a particular comet, which is now named after her. Recently many comets have been discovered and photographed. One is the Comet Hale-Bopp (see http://www2.jpl.nasa.gov/comet/gif/pearson2.jpg). Ask the students to view photos of comets. Make an artistic interpretation of a comet using either black-and-white or colored imagery.

Information Literacy

Objects that can be seen in the night sky include planets, stars or suns, moons, comets, asteroids, gas, dust clouds, and nebulae. Invite the students to find pictures and descriptions of these heavenly bodies on the Internet. The Web sites of the U.S. National Atmospheric and Space Administration have much to offer. See especially http://photojournal.jpl.nasa.gov/index.html.

REFERENCES

Teachers may want to consult:

Gormley, Beatrice. *Maria Mitchell: The Soul of an Astronomer*. Grand Rapids, MI: William B. Eerdmans, 1995.

Maria's Comet

Across

1. A heavenly body made of dust and ice, with a tail.
2. The industry for catching whales.
5. An object that revolves around a planet.
8. An instrument made to enlarge the appearance of distant objects.
10. Italian mathematician and astronomer.
11. A sphere made of hot gases.
12. A scientist who studies the objects in the sky.

Down

1. Patterns of stars in the sky.
3. A small, planet-like object.
4. An early Polish astronomer who believed that the planets orbit the sun.
6. A person who seeks to make discoveries.
7. The North Star.
9. A heavenly body that rotates around a star or sun.

CHAPTER 17

The Desert: *The Tortoise and the Jackrabbit*

Written by Susan Lowell
Flagstaff, AZ: Rising Moon Books, 1994

SUMMARY

This is the perennial favorite story of the turtle and the rabbit as retold in a Southwestern setting.

RELATED CONCEPTS

Animals and humans compete with one another for the opportunity to use natural resources.

The desert environment is home to many specialized plants and animals that can store or find water and shelter in a very hot, dry place.

Adaptations to a dry environment include specialized outer coverings, the ability to live with little water, and the ability to find or make homes underground.

The desert climate includes hot, dry days and cold nights.

RELATED VOCABULARY

badger	mouse
buzzard	quail
coyote	raccoon
elf owl	rattlesnake
frog	roadrunner
gila monster	scorpion
jackrabbit	skunk
javelina	tarantula
kangaroo rat	tortoise

ACTIVITIES

Language Arts

This story is a paraphrase of the old "turtle and the rabbit" fable. Compare this story with another version of the fable for similarities and differences in plot, setting, character, and theme.

Use the graphic organizer in Figure 17.1 to help sequence the events in this story.

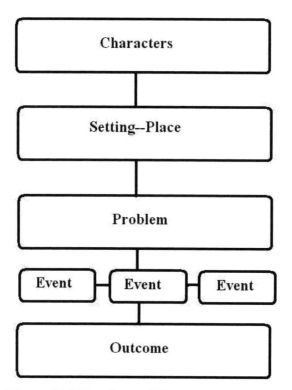

Figure 17.1 *Tortoise and Hare* graphic organizer

Be a reporter at the finish line of this race. Write a newspaper article describing the event. Interview the two main characters for their reactions.

The mesquite tree, which grows in a desert environment, produces a distinctive flavoring, which can be bought as a sauce or in a shaker bottle. Have the students sample small pieces of chicken that have been flavored with mesquite. Give reactions to the flavoring as it is done on television cooking shows.

Social Studies

The setting for this story is probably Arizona or New Mexico (see Figure 17.2). Study a landform map of these states to become familiar with the surface of the land. If possible, contrast these to a precipitation map and a population map. What type of land would you find there? How do precipitation and landforms affect population density? What national parks can be found in these states?

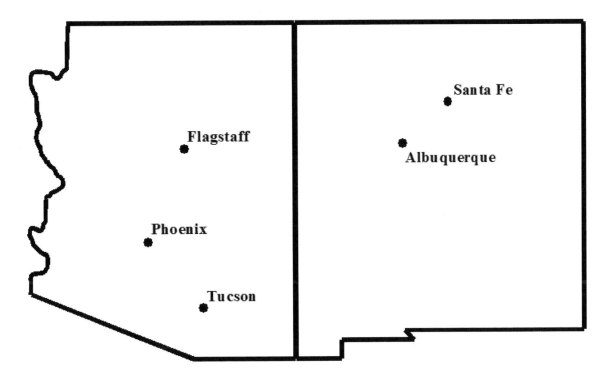

Figure 17.2. Arizona–New Mexico map

Science

Assign each student a desert creature to study. Using reference books or the Internet, have the students write a short description and draw a picture of the creature. Use these in a bulletin board display centered around the maps of Arizona and New Mexico.

The saguaro cactus is sometimes called a "hotel in the desert." What does this phrase mean?

Become familiar with the Saguaro National Park, in the Sonoran Desert. How does this area compare to the background of the tortoise/jackrabbit story?

This story takes place in a desert environment. Make a list of qualifiers for other environments (seashore, mountain, and plains) that can be compared to the desert. Put the qualifiers under the environment they describe. For example, for

Desert	Mountains	Seashore	Plains

These are the qualifiers:

Dry environment

Lack of hills

Snow covered all year

Cactus plants

Abundant rocks

Crossed by many rivers

Temperate climate

Poor soil

110 degrees

Sandy beaches

Tides

Dunes

Joshua trees

Mangrove swamps

High temperatures

Scrubby vegetation

Lack of large lakes

NOTE: Some qualifiers may fit into more than one category.

Mathematics

Assume that this race was five kilometers long. Draw a map of the raceway and the objects that could be seen along the way. Mark the map at one kilometer, two kilometers, etc., using a scale of ten centimeters to a kilometer. Be sure that students understand the length of one kilometer. Practice problems using the metric system as opposed to the English system normally used in this country.

The Arts

There is going to be a rematch between the tortoise and the jackrabbit. Have the students select a favorite animal and make a poster to show their support for that animal.

Use colored chalk to make a sunset scene behind a forest of saguaro cacti.

Information Literacy

A fable is a story that has a moral or lesson. Ask students to locate and read other fables such as Aesop's fables. Have them act out the story and tell the moral.

REFERENCES

There are many variations on the traditional *Aesop's Fable* the "Tortoise and the Hare." The traditional story can be found in the following:

Aesop. *Aesop's Fables*. Hauppauge, NY: Barron's Educational Series, 1989.

Jones, Carol. *The Hare and the Tortoise*. Boston: Houghton Mifflin/Walter Lorraine Books, 1996.

Adaptations

Repchuk, Caroline. *The Race*. San Francisco, CA: Chronicle Books, 2002

Sykes, Julie. *That's Not Fair, Hare!* Hauppauge, NY: Barron's Educational Series, 2001.

www.desertusa.com/animal.html. This is a Web site that provides information about animal adaptations to the desert environment.

The desert tortoise is endangered. Much information about turtles and tortoises is available on the Web site of the California Turtle & Tortoise Club (http://www.tortoise.org/).

The Tortoise and the Jackrabbit

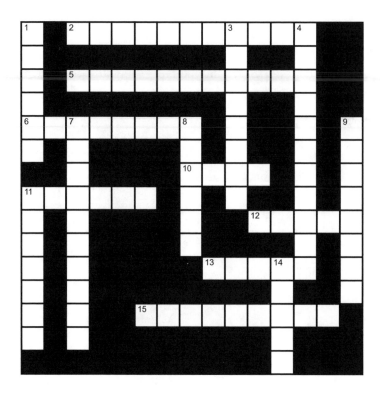

Across

2. A large, poisonous desert lizard.
5. A small rodent.
6. A land turtle.
10. A green, jumping amphibian.
11. A meat-eating, burrowing animal.
12. A wild bird similar to a partridge.
13. A small rodent with a thin tail.
15. A very large, hairy spider.

Down

1. A North American prairie wolf.
3. An animal with claws and a sting in its tail.
4. A poisonous snake with a rattle on its tail.
7. A long-tailed bird that can run very rapidly.
8. A tiny species of owl.
9. A collared peccary—a wild, native, piglike animal.
11. A bird that eats dead animals.
14. A black-and-white animal that gives off a putrid stench.

Part 3
Interactions

CHAPTER 18

Tornadoes: *Twister*

Written by Darleen Bailey Beard
New York: Sunburst Books, Farrar, Straus & Giroux, 2003

SUMMARY

Two small children, Lucille and Natt, experience a tornado as it rips through their neighborhood.

RELATED CONCEPTS

Tornados are funnel-cloud storms that come quickly and can do much damage to a small area.

People are much more likely to survive a tornado if they have and follow a safety plan.

People are most in danger of tornado damage if they are in mobile homes or vehicles.

RELATED VOCABULARY

cone	mobile home
Fujita Scale	rain
funnel cloud	storm cellar
hailstones	thunder
inside hall	vehicle
lightning	window

ACTIVITIES

Language Arts

The coming of a tornado or any natural disaster is a complex event. Ask the students to analyze the events and outcomes of this story using the graphic organizer given in Figure 18.1.

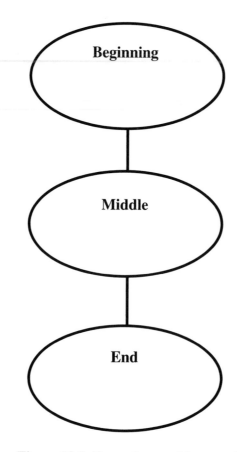

Figure 18.1. Tornado graphic organizer

What are the natural signs that indicated that a tornado was about to strike? At what sign did Mother hurry the children to the storm cellar? Why did she not go down too?

Do the students live in an area where there are tornados? If so, read newspaper clippings about local disasters. Invite someone from the local area who lived through that time to speak about a tornado and its aftermath.

The Xenia, Ohio, tornado on April 3, 1974, is considered to be one of the most widely studied and documented tornados in American history. Using the key words "Xenia, Ohio tornado" on the Internet, find out about this disaster which so profoundly affected the citizens of this city.

Set aside time each day to read *Night of the Twisters* by Ivy Ruckman. This true story took place on June 3, 1980, when eight tornadoes hit Grand Island, Nebraska, on this "night of the twisters."

When a tornado strikes, everyone in the community is affected. Everyone is in need of help, but not everyone can be served immediately. Have the students put on a skit in which students play the part of an electrician, a plumber, a handyman, a building contractor, and the manager of a large building supply store. Have other students represent the following scenarios: the garage is demolished, the porch is ripped off, two trees are down across the driveway, the swing set is demolished, all the windows in house are broken, the family room outside wall is gone, a house has no roof, a boat is blown onto the yard, a tractor-trailer truck is toppled. How will the tradesmen be able to accommodate everyone? Who should be helped first? Will this be an ordinary work week?

Conduct a tornado drill in the school. All students should be seated against inside walls, away from doors and windows. Students pull their knees up under their chins and place an open, hardcover book over their exposed necks. Keep this position until the all clear is sounded. This would be an excellent time to discuss tornado safety rules.

Writing

The children stayed in the storm cellar for a long time. What items do you think should be in the cellar to aid the children? How could they have passed the time away? NOTE: See the American Red Cross emergency list for suggestions.

What thoughts might have gone through Lucille and Natt's minds as they waited in the storm cellar? Write what you think they would feel.

Social Studies

Tornado Alley is a loosely defined term describing those states most likely to suffer from tornado destruction. NOTE: This does not mean that these states always have tornados or that other states, not on the list, are always spared. Locate these states on a map of the United States—Illinois, Indiana, Ohio, Iowa, Missouri, Oklahoma, Kansas, Nebraska, and Texas.

Science

Find out how a tornado is formed and how it causes a path of destruction across the surface of the earth. A very helpful resource on tornadoes is the National Atmospheric and Oceanic Administration (NOAA). See their special Web site at http://www.noaa.gov/tornadoes.html.

Review the actions of Lucille, Natt, their mother, and Mr. Lyle in the period leading up to the tornado and immediately after it. How does their behavior compare with the actions suggested by NOAA and the Red Cross in their guidelines for preparedness? See, for example, http://www.nssl.noaa.gov/NWSTornado/.

A commonly accepted scale, the "Fujita Scale," now assigns a number to the level of damage done by tornadoes (see the table).

The Fujita Scale (Source NOAA)

Number	Intensity	Wind Speed MPH (approximate)	Damage
0	Gale	40–72	Chimneys break, some branches broken, small trees uprooted
1	Moderate	73–112	Roofs are peeled off, mobile homes pushed off foundations or overturned, vehicles pushed off road or overturned
2	Significant	113–157	Entire roofs pulled from homes, mobile homes demolished
3	Severe	158–206	Frame homes demolished, trees snapped or uprooted.
4	Devastating	207–260	Well–constructed homes demolished, Strong frame homes lifted off foundations and moved
5	Incredible	261–318	Nothing constructed by people remains

Which level of the Fujita Scale is probably shown by the tornado in *Twister*? Rate other tornadoes such as those in *Night of the Twister* or those found on NOAA's tornado page.

Mathematics

Make a cone using the pattern in Figure 18.2. Cut out the paper cone and glue it together, matching the tab with the other end of the pattern.

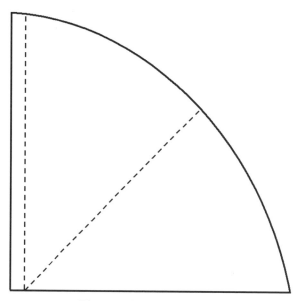

Figure 18.2 Paper cone

Make a graph showing the frequency of tornadoes by state. Figures for an average year from NOAA are given in the following table:

Number of tornadoes per year	State
27	Illinois
23	Indiana
35	Iowa
36	Kansas
27	Missouri
36	Nebraska
16	Ohio
47	Oklahoma
137	Texas

In which state is a person most likely to encounter a tornado on any given day?

The Arts

Have the children make posters to take home outlining the dangers that tornados present and what to do to be prepared if one strikes.

Information Literacy

To access the Internet when searching for information about tornadoes, use the name of the state followed by the word tornado. For example, "Nebraska tornado" gives you charts, tables, graphs, fact sheets, etc., which can be read and interpreted. Other states, for example, for example, "Missouri tornado," will give facts and photos of the destruction. All of the Tornado Alley states can be accessed as well as bordering states.

REFERENCES

Ruckman, Ivy. *Night of the Twisters*. New York: HarperCollins, 1986.

http://www.noaa.gov/tornadoes.html. The official National Atmospheric and Oceanic Administration Web site for tornadoes.

Twister

Across

1. Often heard during a tornado.
5. Electric discharge during a tornado.
7. Safest place in a building during a tornado.
9. Not a safe place on the road during a tornado.
10. A tornado looks like this geometric figure.
11. Could shatter glass during a tornado.
12. Special safe underground place to wait out a tornado.

Down

2. Liquid precipitation that comes with a tornado.
3. The bottom tip of a tornado.
4. Very likely to be damaged by a tornado.
6. A classification for tornadoes.
8. Frozen precipitation that comes with a tornado.

From *The Natural World Through Children's Literature: An Integrated Approach* by Carol M. Butzow and John W. Butzow.
Westport, CT: Libraries Unlimited/Teacher Ideas Press. Copyright © 2007.

CHAPTER 19

Hurricanes: *Hurricane*

Written by David Wiesner
New York: Clarion Books, 1990

SUMMARY

David and George are at home with their parents when a hurricane forecast is heard on the radio. During the night, the storm passes. The next day the boys discover that a big tree has been blown over by the hurricane.

RELATED CONCEPTS

Hurricanes are very dangerous storms with very strong winds.

Hurricanes can greatly damage property and alter lives.

Hurricanes arise over very warm ocean water.

In the North Atlantic, hurricanes often arise off the western coast of Africa and track toward the Gulf of Mexico or the southeastern Atlantic coast of the United States.

RELATED VOCABULARY

condenses	storm surge
counterclockwise	storm track
evaporates	tropical storm
eye	West Africa
rain	wind
solar energy	

ACTIVITIES

Language Arts

Fill in the boxes in the graphic organizer from the story.

A hurricane is a severe cyclone over tropical waters having at least one sustained minute of surface wind of 63 knots (73 mph). Compare this definition with those of tornadoes, cyclones, severe thunderstorms, blizzards, tropical storms, and floods. Are certain kinds of storms prevalent where the students live?

What can we do to protect ourselves from a hurricane? See the American Red Cross pamphlets for suggestions. What did the family in the story do?

Read *Sergio and the Hurricane,* about a young boy who wishes for a hurricane to come until the time when it actually does.

Hurricanes are identified by persons' first names. Is it possible to make a list of hurricane names from A to Z by using names of students, teachers, and school officials? Or personalize your list with sports characters, rock groups, etc.

Writing

Have the students write a biographical piece about a storm that they have personally experienced. It need not be a hurricane.

Have the students create a fantasy about what they would want to find under a tree felled by a hurricane.

As adults, would students prefer to live in areas where hurricanes are quite uncommon or in areas where hurricanes occur quite frequently? Give reasons for this choice.

Social Studies

Locate the major hurricanes named in the following list. What geographical or meteorological conclusions can be drawn from the locations of these storms?

1954	Carol	Northeastern United States
1955	Diane	Eastern United States
1967	Beulah	Texas
1969	Camille	Mississippi and Louisiana
1972	Agnes	Eastern seaboard
1979	David	Eastern U.S
1992	Andrew	Florida
1994	Gordon	Florida
1996	Bertha Eastern	United States
1998	George	Gulf Coast and Florida Keys
1999	Floyd	Eastern seaboard
2005	Katrina	Gulf Coast
2005	Rita	Gulf Coast and Texas
2005	Wilma	Florida

NOTE: Information about major hurricanes can be found in *The World Almanac.*

Have an architect or construction engineer talk to the class about the cost of rebuilding a house after a natural disaster. Is it more economical to start all over with a new property? Is this a financial or emotional decision?

Science

Use the hurricane picture (Figure 19.1) to explain to the class how a hurricane travels across the water from western Africa to the eastern shores of North America. Use the storm-tracking picture (Figure 19.2) to discuss the paths taken by hurricanes in recent years.

Hurricanes get their energy from the intense sunlight that shines over western Africa during the summer months. On an especially sunny day, place plastic dishes of water near the classroom windows in direct sunlight. Using thermometers, keep track of the changes in water temperature due to the solar energy.

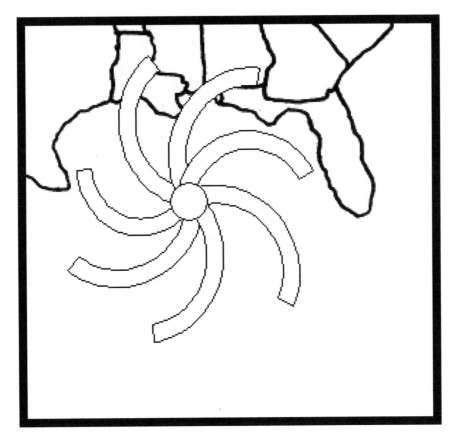

Figure 19.1. Hurricane picture

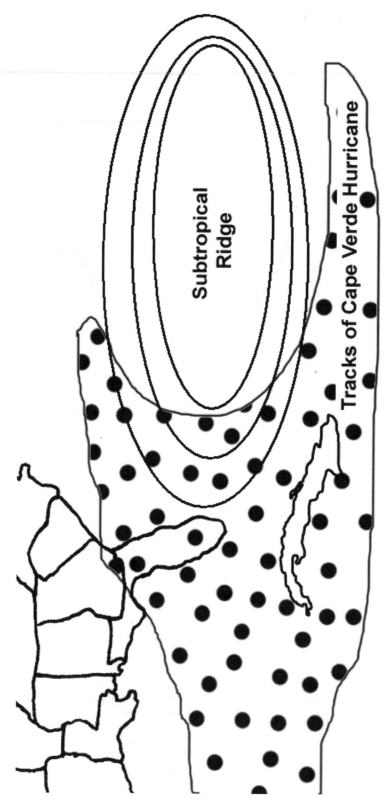

Figure 19.2. Storm-tracking picture

To demonstrate the way heat can cause winds, hold a small paper pinwheel over a candle. Observe the motion of the windmill or pinwheel (see Figure 19.3).

NOTE: This demonstration should be conducted by the teacher only, as fire can result if the paper pinwheel comes too close to the flame.

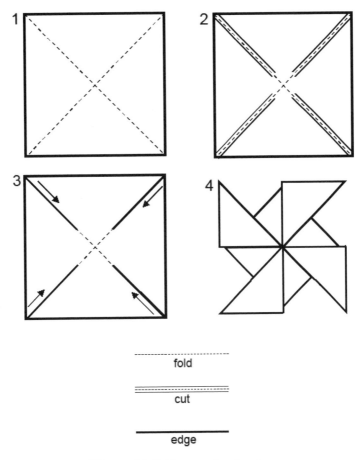

Figure 19.3. Paper pinwheel

Mathematics

The Saffir-Simpson scale is used to categorize hurricanes—Category 1, at 74–95 mph, is weak; Category 2, at 96–110 mph, is moderate; Category 3, at 111–130 mph, is strong; Category 4, at 131–155 mph, is very strong; and Category 5, at over 155 mph, is devastating. Weather forecasters covering the storm will use these categories. Can these speeds be compared to ones the students know—for example,for example, auto speeds, speeds of animals such as the cheetah, airplane flight, etc?

The Arts

Cut apart the matching card game cards (Figure 19.4). Match them to familiarize yourself with the game, than play a regular matching game. Each match of two complementary cards is worth one point.

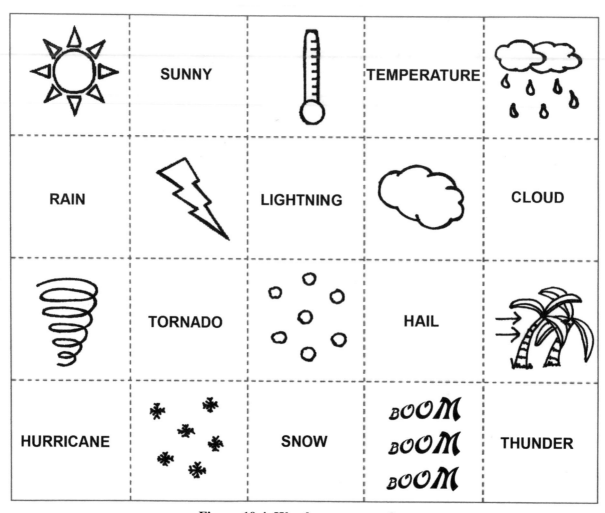

Figure 19.4. Weather game cards

Information Literacy

Since the application of satellite photography to weather forecasting, we have a much better understanding of how hurricanes look and travel over time. The National Oceanographic and Atmospheric Administration of the United States (NOAA) keeps an excellent archive of historically significant images. Children can find and print pictures of many of the hurricanes and other major storms of the recent past.

REFERENCES

http://www5.ncdc.noaa.gov/cgi-bin/hsei/hsei.pl?directive=welcome. This is the Web site for the National Climatic Data Center, part of NOAA. It contains a great many historically significant images of hurricanes and other natural disasters.

Wallner, Alexander. *Sergio and the Hurricane.* New York: Henry Holt, 2000.

Hurricane

Across

1. The huge increase in water level when the hurricane comes ashore.
4. Warm water changes to this vapor as it helps form a storm.
7. Water _____ when it changes back into liquid.
8. It comes with the wind in a hurricane.

Down

2. The path taken as the hurricane moves across the ocean.
3. Center of the hurricane where it is calm.
5. The source of the hurricane's force.
6. The big danger in a hurricane comes from _____.

CHAPTER 20

Conservation Ethics: *Henry Works*

Written by D. B. Johnson
Boston: Houghton Mifflin, 2004

SUMMARY

This is the fourth book in a series about Henry David Thoreau and his love of nature and the simple life.

RELATED CONCEPTS

Thoreau believed in making life simple and uncomplicated.

Thoreau believed that the environment should be treated carefully.

Thoreau expected others to regard nature and natural phenomena as friends and companions.

Thoreau's work was to write about his experiences in the natural world.

RELATED VOCABULARY

Alcott (Louisa May)	mill brook
comfrey root	misty
Concord	mizzling
Emerson (Ralph Waldo)	postmaster
flute	strawberries
Hawthorne (Nathaniel)	Walden Pond
huckleberries	woodchuck

ACTIVITIES

Language Arts

Read other books about Henry David Thoreau such as *Henry Hikes to Fitchburg* and *Henry Builds a Cabin*.

What do we mean by the word *work*? In this book, does Henry "work?" Do children "work?" Can "work" be fun? What is "non-work?" Use a thesaurus to locate synonyms for the word *work*.

Have the class discuss the following lines from *Walden*: "I went to the woods because I wished to live deliberately, to front only the essential facts of life, and see if I could not learn what it had to teach, and not, when I came to die, discover that I had not lived" (p. 80).

Another activist who shared Henry's love of the outdoors was John Muir, who helped set up the National Park System. For more information about this man, read Thomas Locker's *John Muir: America's Naturalist*.

Writing

Conduct a prewriting session before the students are asked to write in their nature books. They should be aware of the importance of observation in what Henry saw, and the rich vocabulary he used to describe things. Impress upon students the use of descriptive words such as adjectives, adverbs, and nouns.

Have the children write their own "nature books" recounting their experiences on a nature walk or viewing a nature video. What observations were made? Use illustrations as well as text.

Have the students think about what Henry's home would be like with no modern conveniences. Select one of two scenarios for a writing sample—for example, I would like to live as Henry did, or I would prefer living in the world as it is today. Give several reasons for the choice.

Social Studies

Look at the map on the inside page of the cover. Use the information on the map to answer the following questions:

In which direction does the Sudbury River flow?

Into which body of water does the river flow?

Which two rivers combine to form the Sudbury?

What are the names of Henry's four friends whose houses are pictured here?

Which friend lives closest to the Sudbury River?

At which building did Henry stop when he was in town?

Henry's cabin adjoins this body of water.

What form of public transportation runs through Concord?

Henry often does not take the roads through the town. Why is this so?

What is a turnpike?

Which appears to be longer—the Nut Meadows Stream or the Mill Stream?

Look at the illustrations in the book. Approximately when did Henry live? For example, look at the picture inside his cabin. What energy source do you see being used?

NOTE: Thoreau lived from 1817 to 1862.

Science

The main theme of Henry's books is the observation of nature. What does he learn from the plants? From the landscape? From the weather?

How did Henry know a storm was coming? What signs help predict a change in the weather? What are some other weather sayings—for example, "Red skies at night, sailors' delight; red skies in the morning, sailors take warning." Find other weather sayings on the Internet.

Organize a walk in the woods or on a nature trail. Or obtain a video that portrays an experience outdoors. What do the students observe—for example, plants, animals, etc.? What inferences can be made? What conclusions can be drawn?

Henry tended his garden faithfully. Grow a small container garden in the classroom. Quick-sprouting vegetables include radishes and squash. Quick-sprouting flowers include marigolds and nasturtiums. Or start an herb garden that can be placed in a sunny window (see Figure 20.1).

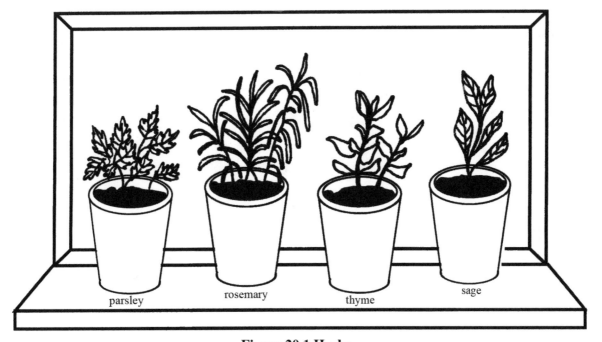

Figure 20.1 Herbs

Mathematics

The scale of miles on the map on the inside cover of *Henry Works* is approximately one inch equals ⅓ mile or .3 mile. Use this figure to find out the answers to the following questions.

a) How far must Henry walk to go from his cabin to Emerson's house? NOTE: There are two possible ways.

b) How far is it from Henry's cabin to downtown Concord, Massachusetts?

c) How far is it from Alcott's house to Hawthorne's home?

d) Which is closer to the post office—Henry's cabin or Hosmer's house?

e) When Henry went to the strawberry fields, he was closest to the home of this friend.

f) How far is it from the village church to the railroad station?

Have students create additional questions.

Study a modern-day road map. Use the scale of miles or the numbering system alongside the road to figure how far Henry is from Fitchburg, Boston, Lexington, Cambridge, or other cities in the area. How long would it take to walk these distances if you can walk ten miles a day?

The Arts

Many contemporary organizations work for the preservation of our natural resources. Often they express this philosophy with the use of logos on T-shirts and other articles of clothing, posters, bumper stickers, etc. Have a competition in which the students design a logo advocating the wise use and preservation of our natural resources. Investigate the cost of producing T-shirts bearing the winning logo for all the students. (See Figure 20.2.)

Henry's cabin was 10-by-15 feet. Make a floor plan to show where he might keep things.

Figure 20.2 Conservation T-shirt

Information Literacy

Find the Web site for Concord, Massachusetts. Compare this present-day city to the nineteenth-century town where Henry lived.

REFERENCES

Locker, Thomas. *John Muir: America's Naturalist*. Golden, CO: Fulcrum Publishing, 2003. A wonderful children's book about the first public advocate for national parks.

http://www.dbjohnsonart.com/artist/. Web site for information about the author, D.B. Johnson.

Thoreau, Henry David. *Walden or Life in the Woods*. New York: Alfred A. Knopf—Everyman's Library, 1910.

Johnson has written additional books depicting Thoreau:

Johnson, D. B. *Henry Builds a Cabin*. Boston: Houghton Mifflin, 2002

Johnson, D. B. *Henry Climbs a Mountain*. Boston: Houghton Mifflin, 2003.

Johnson, D. B. *Henry Hikes to Fitchburg*. Boston: Houghton Mifflin, 2000.

The State of Massachusetts has preserved the site of Thoreau's cabin and has erected a replica on the site. For more information, the park Web site is http://www.mass.gov/dcr/parks/northeast/wldn.htm.

Henry Works

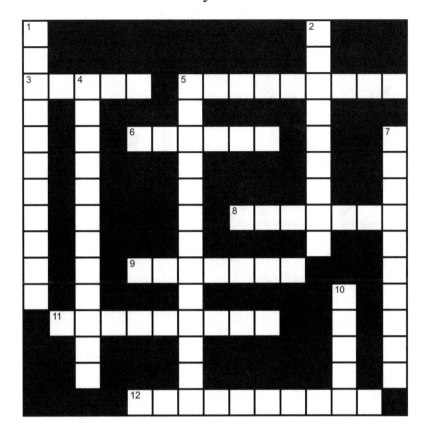

Across

3. Foggy.

5. He wrote the *Scarlet Letter*.

6. She wrote *Little Women*.

8. A town in Massachusetts near Lexington.

9. A famous eighteenth-century author who believed in self-reliance.

11. The stream where Henry waded to watch the water level during a rainstorm.

12. The person in charge of the local post office.

Down

1. An herb used to sooth athletic injuries, bruises, burns, and dry skin.

2. Groundhogs are often pests to farmers and gardeners.

4. Wonderful tasting red ground berries.

5. These are pretty much the same thing as blueberries.

7. The place where Henry built his cabin in the woods.

10. Henry played this instrument, like the Pied Piper of Hamlin

CHAPTER 21

Drought and Survival: *The Water Hole*

Written by Graeme Base
New York: Puffin Books, 2001

SUMMARY

A well-visited water hole eventually dries up, making it necessary for the animals to go elsewhere or perish.

RELATED CONCEPTS

Water is essential to all living things.

Many parts of the world have wet and dry seasons rather than hot and cold seasons.

Animals respond differently to dry weather.

RELATED VOCABULARY

drinking	lumbering
floundering	meeting
gazing	sipping
lapping	squawking
looking	wallowing

ACTIVITIES

Language Arts

Each page in this book uses a very powerful verb or action word. Have the students learn the meanings of these words and be able to use them in a game of Simon Says.

What is the significance of the water drying up? What would happen if the water supply in your town dried up or became dangerously low? How could students help spread the news to conserve water?

Writing

Have each student make a report on one of the animals in the border strip of each page.

Imagine you are a tiger and the water in the pond is lower each day when you go to drink. What would you do? What would the toucan do? What would the tortoise do? What would the kangaroo do? How do humans react to a change in water availability?

Are there ESL or other students who can teach the class to count from 1 to 10 in another language? Are these animals named differently in that country?

Social Studies

Locate the countries or continents where the animals lived. Silhouettes and names of the animals can be put on the bulletin board or wall chart along with the name of each country or continent (see Figure 21.1).

Figure 21.1. Animal silhouettes

In some areas of the world monsoon rains are awaited as a source of water. This is called the wet or rainy season. These include countries in Southeast Asia, India, Africa, Australia, and Malaysia. Locate these monsoon areas.

Science

Fill a clear plastic container to the rim with water. Let the container sit undisturbed for several days. Check the water level each day. Where does the water go?

Have the students discuss and illustrate the steps in the water cycle—that is, the rain runs in to rivers and streams; the waterways flow into the ocean; the water is heated by the sun and evaporates; and the water vapor rises to the clouds, where it is cooled and falls again as rain.

If possible, visit a pond and observe the wildlife in the area. Are there signs of animals in the area? Are there plants growing near the water? Observe and describe what you see. Is there evidence that the water level ever changes in the pond? DVDs or videos may be available to provide this information.

What can be deduced from the movement of animals? Observe pets, backyard wildlife, or zoo Web cams on the Internet, for example, http://nationalzoo.si.edu/Animals/AfricanSavanna/default.cfm?cam=C3.

Mathematics

Temperate climates of the earth have consistently wet and dry areas. In *The World Almanac*, look up the precipitation for cities in the United States and graph them by month. Be sure to include dry areas such as Phoenix, Arizona, and Dallas, Texas, and wet areas such as Portland, Oregon, and Seattle, Washington. The same activity can be done using almanac statistics for cities of the world—for example, Hong Kong, China, and Lima, Peru. NOTE: An average rainfall would be about 30 to 50 inches of precipitation in temperate climates.

The Arts

Make a series of storyboards showing what happens to the area of the water hole as it dries up.

Invent an animal that can store up large amounts of water in its body.

Information Literacy

What is an extinct animal? Observe the extinct animals on the page where the water has disappeared. Check the Internet for other animals that have become extinct. What are the reasons those animals are no longer living? What is the difference between extinct, endangered, and threatened animals?

Find out about organizations that attempt to save animals from extinction—for example, the World Wildlife Fund or the Sierra Club.

REFERENCES

http://www.worldwildlife.org/. This is the Web site of the World Wildlife Fund, which sponsors projects to help save wildlife worldwide.

http://www.sierraclub.org/. The Sierra Club is another organization that advocates for protection of the environment.

The Water Hole

Across

   5. Making a loud, harsh sound.

   8. Taking in very small amounts of liquid.

   9. Moving clumsily.

  10. Looking long and steadily.

Down

   1. Directing the eyes.

   2. Moving in a slow, heavy way.

   3. Gathering with others.

   4. Swallowing liquid.

   6. Rolling about in water.

   7. Taking in liquid with the tongue.

CHAPTER 22

The Cloud Forest Environment:
The Umbrella

Written by Jan Brett
New York: Putnam, 2004

SUMMARY

A young boy spends a day in the cloud forest looking for the elusive quetzal bird and other animals.

RELATED CONCEPTS

The cloud forest is a tropical mountain evergreen forest where clouds cover the treetops almost all of the time.

The humidity in a cloud forest is very nearly 100 percent all of the time.

In cloud forests, as in all rain forests, a great deal of the animal activity occurs at the treetop or canopy level.

In a cloud forest, the precipitation does not fall down but gathers like dew from the clouds as they touch the treetops.

RELATED VOCABULARY

frog	monkey
hummingbird	quetzal
jaguar	tapir
kinkajou	toucan

ACTIVITIES

Language Arts

Read other books by author Jan Brett. What type of characters does she use? Where do her stories often take place?

Animals in this book are given human characteristics, or they are personified. These animals include the jaguar, monkey, tapir, toucan, kinkajou, frog, quetzal, and hummingbird. Learn several facts about each animal.

People in Costa Rica are known for their love of the theater. Rewrite this book as a play starring the little boy, his father, and the animals.

Learn some Spanish phrases from the book—for example, *Buena sweete*—Good luck; *Que pasa?*—What's happening?; *No problema*—No problem; *Adios*—Goodbye.

Writing

Civilization is constantly encroaching on areas like the cloud forest. Have the students explain their opinions about developing the cloud forest or leaving it as it is.

Social Studies

Cloud forests exist from Panama to Argentina. Locate this land mass and determine which continents are represented. Locate Costa Rica, where the story takes place.

On a map of Costa Rica (Figure 22.1), label the bodies of water and other countries that touch this one.

Figure 22.1 Map of Costa Rica

Science

The cloud forest is an ecosystem in and of itself, where the humidity is usually 100 percent. It is independent of the rain forest and usually rises from 5,000 feet to 10,000 feet in altitude. Altitude and temperature account for the cloud forest's existence above the rain forest.

Air rises and moisture condenses. Students may re-create a similar phenomenon by placing a cold, filled soda can on the table. In a few minutes, moisture will form as the air is cooled by the soda can. Or place zippered bags of ice on each student's desk. NOTE: This is part of the water cycle in which water vapor rises, condenses, and falls as rain.

Web cams can be utilized to hear the sounds of the cloud forest animals. Describe these voices. Can they be replicated by the students?

From the Internet, obtain photos of animals that live in the area, especially the quetzal, which can be colored a variety of shades.

The fig tree is often mentioned in the book. Look up a fig tree in a book of trees or houseplants.

Mathematics

Costa Rica consists of 19,730 square miles. Using *The World Almanac*, compare this to the size of the students' state. Costa Rica is closest in size to West Virginia. Which is larger?

Sequence the animals in the story in order of size. Make cutouts to represent the animals.

The Arts

Make a mural or board display that can be used as a backdrop for the play that the students will produce. Various hats can be used to represent the animals.

Information Literacy

Cloudforestalive.com presents a quiz to see how much the reader already knows about the cloud forest. What scores do the students receive?

REFERENCES

www.centralamerica.com/cr/info/. Costa Rica tourist Web site provides maps and information about the country.

www.monteverdeinfo.com/. The Web site of the Monteverde, Costa Rica, cloud forest.

www.cloudforestalive.org/. The Web site of the Tropical Science Center, a nonprofit group that sponsors educational and scientific study of the Monteverde cloud forest.

http://www.explorehonduras.com/cloudforest2.htm. This travel Web site details the cloud forests of Honduras, a neighboring country to Costa Rica.

The Umbrella

Across

2. A furry primate.
4. A bird with a large, yellow bill.
7. A large, spotted cat.
8. A small, brightly colored bird that feeds on flower nectar.

Down

1. An intense green rain forest bird with long tail feathers.
3. A funny, furry animal.
5. It has a long nose and is related to the rhino.
6. A green, jumping amphibian.

CHAPTER 23

Lightning and Electricity:
How Ben Franklin Stole the Lightning

Written by Rosalyn Schanzer
New York: HarperCollins, 2003

SUMMARY

Many of Franklin's ideas and inventions are showcased in this book. One of the most important was his experiment to prove that lightning is electricity.

RELATED CONCEPTS

Electricity is a form of energy that is conducted most easily through metals.

Static electricity can be generated by friction.

Electricity can be seen as sparks.

Lightning is a very strong charge of static electricity.

RELATED VOCABULARY

fire	lightning rod
Gulf Stream	metal
key	rubbing
kite	spark
lightning	stove

ACTIVITIES

Language Arts

Give the name of one of Franklin's inventions to each student to research—for example, the Franklin stove, the bifocal, the lightning rod, the postal system, etc. How would life in the twenty-first century be different without these items or services?

Is it possible for people to be injured or killed in an electrical storm? Study the American Red Cross pamphlet on how to survive a thunder and lightning storm.

The Weather Channel can be consulted for up-to-the-minute information about an oncoming storm. Also, local weather forecasts are helpful. Have the students jot down the information from an evening forecast. Compare that information to the actual weather of the next day.

As "Poor Richard," Franklin showered the public with his proverbs. Select several of these from the Internet and let each students illustrate and explain the chosen proverb—for example, "An apple a day keeps the doctor away," "There are no gains without pains," "A penny saved is a penny earned," etc.

Writing

I would like to work with Ben Franklin and help him invent a (an) _____. Give reasons for the need for this invention and how it would work. Include a drawing.

Social Studies

Franklin was born in Boston, Massachusetts, then moved to Philadelphia, Pennsylvania, where he resided for many years. He also lived on assignment in London, England, and Paris, France. Locate these cities on the world map (see Figure 1.2). Discuss the reasons that took Benjamin Franklin to Europe for so many years. Why did he return in 1775?

Franklin lived in London from 1752 to 1775, and the building where he lived has been preserved (see www.benjaminfranklinhouse.org).

Science

Franklin worked with static electricity. We can experience static electricity by rubbing a two- or three-foot-long piece of ¾-inch plastic pipe with wool cloth or a wool scarf. Notice that when the pipe is vigorously rubbed, a crackling sound is created. Test the power of the charged plastic pipe by picking up small pieces of paper. (See Figures 23.1 and 23.2.)

Figure 23.1. Electrifying a plastic pipe

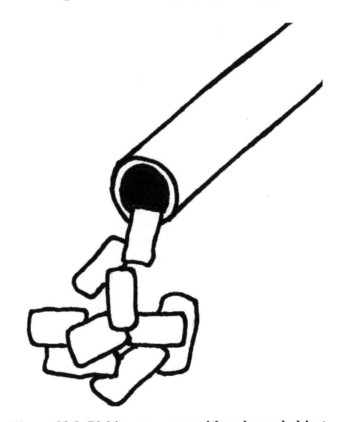

Figure 23.2. Picking up paper with a charged object

A static electric charge can be "stored" in a way that Franklin perfected. Follow the directions in Figure 23.3 to line the inside of a small plastic kitchen container with aluminum foil. Make a small hole in the lid and insert a screw through the hole. Attach a wire to the top of the screw and another to the bottom. With the lined container assembled, vigorously rub the pipe with the scarf near the wire attached to the top of the container. Put down the pipe, and using something nonmetallic like a wooden pencil, bring the wire attached to the side of the container toward but not touching the head of the screw, which protrudes from the top of the container. Usually there is a small spark formed as the wire comes close. This is a direct way to observe electricity. NOTE: Students may experience a shock while petting an animal or changing clothes.

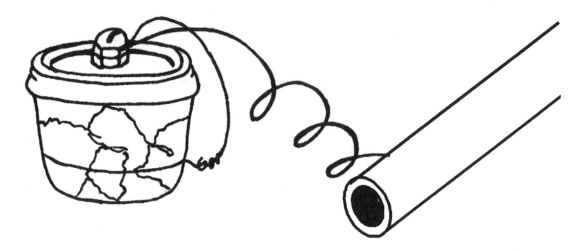

Figure 23.3. Making a spark from a charged object

Mathematics

Franklin was very fond of mathematics and mathematical games. One of his favorite pastimes was to create "magic squares," in which the rows always added up to the same number (in this case 8). Have the children generate rules to explain what was done.

3	4	1
4	4	0
2	2	4

Have the students create squares and exchange them with each other to see if the partner can guess the number that will solve the problem.

Some students may wish to experiment with squares with more than three columns for each row and can also create squares where the columns and rows both add up to the same number.

The Arts

Divide a sheet of drawing paper into four sections. In the center, draw a picture of Franklin. In each corner of the paper, draw one of Franklin's inventions or an important event in his life. Post these in the hallway for others to enjoy.

Information Literacy

There are a great many Web pages that show pictures of Franklin's early electrical equipment. Have students make a class collection of the electronic images and create a way to show the results for the whole class, for example, a series of digital pictures or a slide show.

REFERENCES

Teachers may want to consult the following books:

Brands, H. W. *The First American: The Life and Times of Benjamin Franklin*. New York: Anchor Books, 2002.

Morgan, Edmund S. *Benjamin Franklin*. New Haven, CT: Yale University Press, 2002.

Much information about Benjamin Franklin is available from the Franklin Institute in Philadelphia. The Web site is http://www.fi.edu.

How Ben Franklin Stole the Lightning

Across

1. The best conductors of electricity are _____.
3. What Franklin stole from the sky.
6. It helps generate static electricity.
7. Franklin used a _____ to get his string into the sky.
8. Franklin's invention to help home heating.

Down

2. It conducts lightning away from a building.
4. A warm current in the Atlantic Ocean
5. The common result of lightning striking a house.
7. It was attached to the kite string.
8. Evidence that electricity has passed through the air.

CHAPTER 24

Mangrove Islands:
The Sea, the Storm, and the Mangrove Tangle

Written by Lynne Cherry

New York: Farrar, Straus & Giroux, 2004

SUMMARY

The life cycle of the mangrove tree gives an intimately detailed look at a tropical environment.

RELATED CONCEPTS

Mangroves exist in salty tropical seas where they can extract the salt out of the sea water.

Mangroves give off propagules, which allow the seeds to float many miles away before a new plant is established.

Mangroves provide a safe place for sea animals, fish, and birds to weather storms.

RELATED VOCABULARY

algae	manatees
anole lizards	mangrove snappers
Caribbean	mangrove tree crab
dolphin	pelican
fiddler crab	periwinkle
frigate bird	pollinated
grunts	prop roots
hawk	propagule
hummingbirds	sea grass
hurricane	seahorse
lagoon	shrimp

ACTIVITIES

Language Arts

Read *The Great Kapok Tree* and *A River Ran Wild,* both by Lynne Cherry. What is her view of nature and the environment? Does this book follow a similar theme?

Have students select an animal from the inside cover of the book to research. Try to find three or four facts about the animal and make a sketch that can be put on a bulletin board.

Writing

What is unacceptable about the following statement? "After the hurricane, there was no damage done—just a few mangroves were destroyed."

Explain what is meant when mangroves are referred to as "the nursery of the ocean floor."

Social Studies

Mangroves exist on five continents. Which continents are they? Where do mangroves exist in North America? List other nations that have mangroves.

Science

Compare a mangrove tree to a normal shade tree that would be found in a temperate climate. How are they alike? How are they different?

Grow your own mangrove plant. Small plants can be purchased from the TopTropical Company and grown in small glass containers. They suggest that you fill a one-gallon glass globe container about two-thirds with glass ornamental marbles and water. Place the mangrove upright and position it with the marbles. Fertilize with dilute liquid plant food. (See Figure 24.1.)

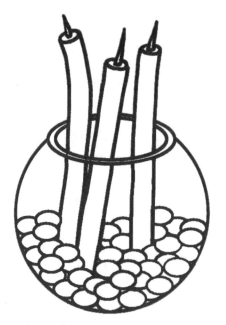

Figure 24.1 Planting a mangrove

Ask the students to classify the animals in the book as invertebrates, fish, amphibians, reptiles, birds, or mammals. The animals are dolphins, pelicans, tree crabs, egrets, coral, anole lizards, manatees, oysters, fiddler crabs, sea anemones, tree snails, hummingbirds, hawks, herons, seahorses, shrimp, fish, mangrove snappers, caterpillars, and frigate birds. Other animals can be found on the inside cover of the book.

Mathematics

This book gives certain highlights in the life of a mangrove—for example, the mangrove can live to be 100 years old. Make a timeline that gives other highlights in the life of the mangrove.

The Arts

Pantomime what happens to a mangrove during a hurricane. Have students act out the part of the mangroves as well as the animals that find shelter there. How does the mangrove protect the animals?

Information Literacy

Mangrove islands and swamps are endangered throughout the world. There are groups working to restore the mangrove. Locate the Web sites for these groups and learn the steps they are taking to help restore the mangroves. Use the key words, "save the mangroves."

REFERENCES

Cherry, Lynne. *A River Ran Wild.* New York: Harcourt Brace Jovanovich, 1992.

Cherry, Lynne. *The Great Kapok Tree.* New York: Harcourt Brace Jovanovich, 1990.

http://www.toptropicals.com/html/aqua/plants/mangrove/mangrove_eng.htm. This Web site provides information about growing mangroves indoors.

http://ology.amnh.org/marinebiology/workthesystem/seaofquestions.html. A Web site operated by the American Museum of Natural History dealing with mangroves.

The Sea, the Storm, and the Mangrove Tangle

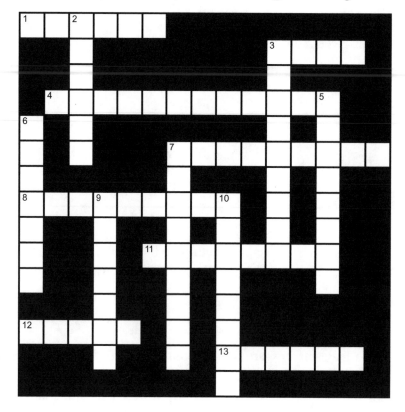

Across

1. A shallow body of salt water.
3. A medium-sized bird of prey.
4. Slender, climbing lizards with sticky toes.
7. To apply pollen to make the seed develop.
8. Special roots that help hold up the tree trunk.
11. A sea animal also called a sea cow.
12. Seaweed that often grows attached to mangrove roots
13. A small crustacean that becomes pink when cooked.

Down

2. A foot-long fish that makes a grunting sound.
3. A very large and violent storm with cyclone winds.
5. A grass that is adapted to live underwater in salt water environments.
6. A streamlined sea animal like a porpoise.
7. The part of the mangrove that detaches itself to allow the seeds to float away.
9. Large, brown sea bird with a huge bill to carry fish.
10. A small saltwater fish that resembles a horse.

From *The Natural World Through Children's Literature: An Integrated Approach* by Carol M. Butzow and John W. Butzow. Westport, CT: Libraries Unlimited/Teacher Ideas Press. Copyright © 2007.

CHAPTER 25

Stream Ecology: *Crawdad Creek*

Written by Scott Russell Sanders
Washington, DC: National Geographic Society, 1999

SUMMARY

A girl and her brother experience the creek behind their home.

RELATED CONCEPTS

The life in the creek adapts to different conditions.

Many different forms of life inhabit the creek.

The creek attracts different animals depending on climatic conditions.

The creek bed contains a variety of rocks, fossils, and soils.

RELATED VOCABULARY

arrowhead	minnow
bullhead	monarch butterfly
crayfish	nuggets
damselfly	salamander
dragonfly	snail
fossil	snake
frog	tracks
gravel	turtle
kingfisher	

ACTIVITIES

Language Arts

Before reading the book, ask the students, "What is a creek?" Record the answers. Read the book and ask the same question. How do students now define the word? How is it different from a pond, a stream, or a brook? NOTE: There is no specific definition for the word "creek."

There are many words to describe the way water flows in a creek. Investigate the various ways these words (and other words) make students visualize water flow: drift, flood, flow, rush, gush, surge, run, pour, course, circulate, and ripple. When they close their eyes and listen to these words, what do they "see" in their mind's eye?

Writing

The girl in the story says that she is never lonesome at Crawdad Creek because, "The water keeps talking." Have the students explain what Lizzie meant. Then write about a place where they feel at peace with the world—perhaps a bedroom, a wooded area, a spot near a body of water, etc.

Many animals are described in the book. Have each student select one to study and illustrate. Are these animals helpful to people, or are they a nuisance? Where do the creatures fit into a drawing of the food chain (Figure 25.1)?

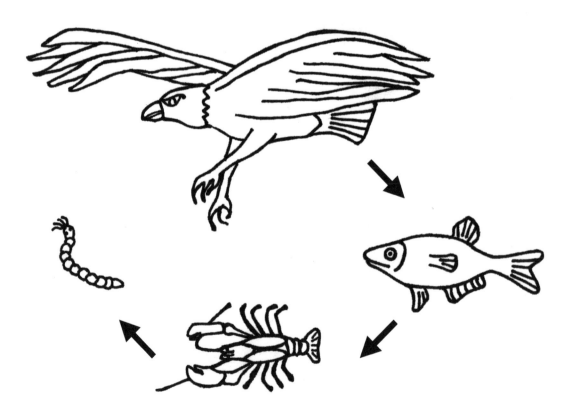

Figure 25.1. Food chain diagram

Social Studies

The children in the story found a relic of a past culture—a Native American arrowhead. If the students live in an area that was once inhabited by Native Americans, ask a speaker to talk about the culture of that particular ethnic group. A local history museum may be able to supply or suggest a speaker and provide a collection of artifacts to view.

Science

If it is possible, take the children on a field trip so that they can see, hear, and touch a creek. Be sure to provide at least one adult leader for each group of three children. Before going, establish rules for behavior to ensure that no one enters the creek or behaves in an unsafe manner.

Select several fifty-foot sections of the creek for detailed investigation. Have the class record the obstacles to the water flow as well as the natural structures that allow shade and hiding places for fish and other animals that live in the water. Ask the adult volunteer leaders to assist in making a large sketched map of the part of the creek selected for study (see Figure 25.2). Make measurements and a key to locate each important observation. You may want to borrow a wheel measurer from the athletic department to use to measure the fifty-foot sections (see Figure 25.3).

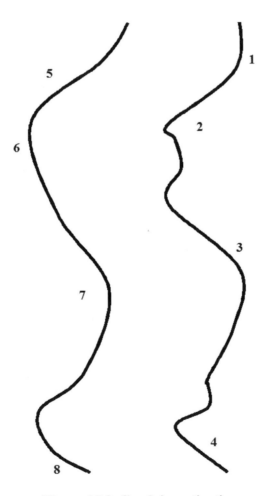

Figure 25.2. Creek investigations

Figure 25.3. Measuring wheel

For the math activity below, have groups note the following for their specific study site:

Study Site Number	
Number of Living Things • Crayfish • Fish • Beetles • Flying Insects	
Time for a small twig to flow five feet along the creek	
Type of creek bed material	
Obstacles to water flow	
Fossils found	
Shade or hiding places	
Other interesting observations	

Fill several small bottles with creek water to be analyzed in the classroom using microscopes or hand lenses.

The fossils in the book were brachiopods and gastropods. Obtain samples of these two creatures from a biological supply house. Have the students examine these fossils and try to reconstruct their lives. Internet findings can provide information and drawings for this task. If you find fossils on your field trip, consult the *Golden Guide to Fossils* for assistance in further investigating the fossil.

Using topographical maps, locate a creek near to the students' homes. Follow this stream as it flows into larger bodies of water and eventually to the ocean. NOTE: A series of maps will probably be necessary to do this. Information about topographical maps of your areas can be obtained online from the U.S. Geological Survey (http://education.usgs.gov/common/primary.htm#topographic). There are online services that will allow you to see sections of a topographical map and will search by a place name such as "Two Lick Creek." One such service is http://www.topozone.com.

Choose one student from each group who have spent time at the site of a creek and have them form a panel to share their experiences with the class. A parent volunteer might also tell his or her story and bring water back for the students to study.

How does a creek fit into the water cycle?

Crayfish (crawdads) can be purchased from a biological supply company or in some cases, a seafood shop, and kept alive for some time in a large tub in the classroom. Consult science supply houses such as Carolina Biological Supply Company (http://www.carolina.com) for living specimens. Be sure to order well in advance and let the vendor know when you want to use them in the classroom. Most vendors sell food for the crayfish as well.

Mathematics

Using data collected by each group of three students, record their data for stream flow, numbers and types of living things observed, and other conditions such as exposure of the creek to sunlight or shade. Develop generalizations about the kinds of living things you would expect to find at the creek based on the variables of flow rate and sunny or shady or sheltered area.

The Arts

Crawdads are decapods (deca = ten, pod = foot), along with lobsters, which have ten appendages counting the legs and claws (five on each side). Have the students draw cartoon versions of a decapod including all ten appendages (see Figure 25.4).

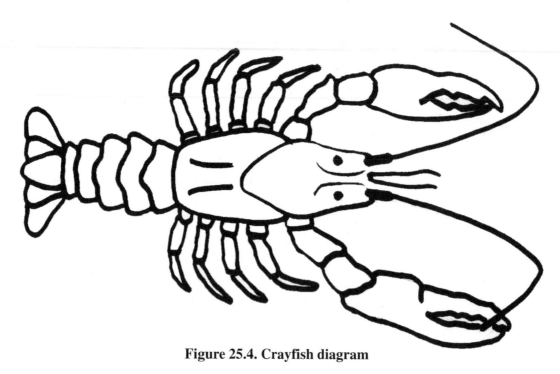

Figure 25.4. Crayfish diagram

Information Literacy

Ask the class to learn more about people who have interests in creeks and streams. Consult the Web sites of organizations known to be supportive of conservation of creeks and streams, such as the Isaac Walton League of America (http://www.iwla.org) and Trout Unlimited (http://www.tu.org). Web pages from state and regional fisheries departments may also be able to provide information about good ways to promote the health of brooks, creeks, streams, and other small bodies of moving water in your region.

REFERENCES

Cottam, Clarence. *Insects, Revised Edition*. New York: Golden Guides from St. Martin's Press, 2001.

Reid, George K. *Pond Life, Revised Edition*. New York: Golden Guides from St. Martin's Press, 2001.

Rhodes, Frank H. T. *Fossils, Revised Edition*. New York: Golden Guides from St. Martin's Press, 2001.

Smith, Hobart M. *Reptiles and Amphibians, Revised Edition*. New York: Golden Guides from St. Martin's Press, 2001.

Crawdad Creek

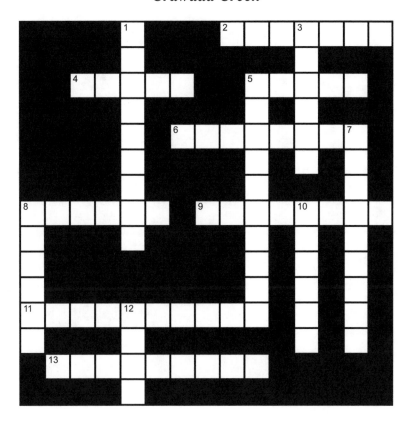

Across

2. Small nodules of precious metal.
4. A crawling reptile.
5. A shellfish with one larger shell.
6. A fish with barbells.
8. A reptile with an armored shell.
9. A freshwater crustacean.
11. A large-headed, belted bird that hovers over water.
13. Native Americans made these.

Down

1. A large, flying insect with two sets of wings.
3. A typical stream bed material.
5. A shy amphibian that walks on all fours.
7. Smaller and more delicate than a dragonfly.
8. Prints left by passing animals.
10. Preserved remains of living things in rock.
12. An amphibian that is adapted to jump.

CHAPTER 26

Trash and Garbage Disposal: *I Stink*

Written by Kate and Jim McMullan
New York: HarperCollins, 2002

SUMMARY

The job of being a garbage truck is presented in spectacular and "trashy" detail.

RELATED CONCEPTS

Garbage trucks are at work while people are asleep.

Garbage bags are compacted to make room for additional trash/garbage.

Garbage trucks are very powerful to handle the job they must do.

People depend on garbage trucks and their drivers to collect trash/garbage.

Trash/garbage must be disposed of in a more permanent manner.

RELATED VOCABULARY

blade	pistons
brakes	reverse
compacted	sanitation
doubles	steering wheel
eject	tail gate
engine	throttle
gas pedal	trash
hopper	

ACTIVITIES

Language Arts

Interview the building custodian concerning the work that is involved in keeping the school clean. What methods of disposal are used? How much trash/garbage is generated by the entire school district? What money must be allocated for this purpose?

After reading the "Trashy ABCs" in this book, have the students compile their own list of ABCs.

Another story similar in content to *I Stink* is *Trashy Town* by Andrea Zimmerman and David Clemesha.

Writing

Have students describe how they can cut down the amount of material that is thrown away in the school. Do any of the disposable items qualify for recycling? Can items be compacted before disposal—for example, cardboard boxes.

Social Studies

Using the yellow pages of a local directory, locate the various trash/garbage collection businesses. How do they dispose of their trash—landfill, open dumps, burning, recycling, etc.? Is this system environmentally appropriate? Is there a possibility of making this system less likely to pollute the environment?

Is there a recycling depot in the area? Is this town managed, or a volunteer system? What items are collected? Are they actually recycled, or deposited in with other trash/garbage? What items can be made from recycled products?

Science

Household trash/garbage is generally removed from the home once a week. How does one get rid of larger items such as a couch, a computer, a mattress, etc? Contact local trash/garbage companies to see how this is accomplished.

Trash/garbage, when sealed in bags, tends to trap gas. To determine what happens to gas as it is heated, try this as a teacher demonstration. Inflate a balloon and tie off the end securely so air cannot escape. Now place the balloon in a basin of warm water. What happens to the balloon? Try the same thing with a basin of ice water. As gas is heated, what happens to its volume?

Mathematics

With the help of the custodian, find out how much trash/garbage a school generates in a week. For example, if each room produces two bags of trash/garbage per day X five days a week X twenty rooms, how many bags is that? Bags may then be transferred to a garbage truck, which could represent a total figure for the week's trash. Some schools may have a specific-sized dumpster to collect the bags and determine the total amount of trash/garbage for the week.

Obtain copies of trash/garbage bills from local companies. What is the cost of a weekly/monthly collection? Is there a limit to the amount of trash/garbage that is put out for pickup? Is trash/garbage to be bagged or left in large plastic containers? Is there any recycling of items—for example, newspapers, bottles, etc

The Arts

Collect clean but unwanted items to make a three-dimensional collage—for example, small toys, art supplies, game pieces, broken jewelry, etc. Glue them onto a foot- square piece of cardboard. Paint the piece with a single color of acrylic paint.

Information Literacy

Learn more about how garbage trucks are made. Make a classroom display of garbage truck pictures. See, for example, the Heil Company Web site (http://www.heil.com/products/pythonmulti.asp). (See Figures 26.1 and 26.2.)

Figure 26.1. Garbage truck foldout

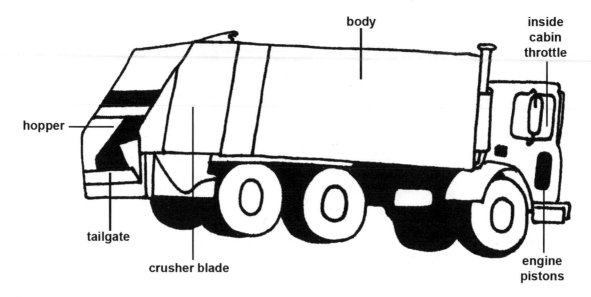

body

inside cabin throttle

hopper

tailgate

crusher blade

engine pistons

Figure 26.2. Garbage truck parts

REFERENCES

Harlow, Rosie. *Garbage and Recycling.* (Young Discoverers: Environmental Facts and Experiments). New York: Kingfisher Books, 2002.

Zimmerman, Andrea, and David Clemesha. *Trashy Town.* New York: HarperCollins, 1999.

I Stink

Across

3. The drivers use these to stop the truck.
5. The part of the inside of the engine where the fuel is burned.
7. The source of energy and power for the garbage truck.
8. To push out.
10. The door on the back of the truck that keeps the garbage in.
11. Anything we want to throw away.
12. The gear that moves the truck backwards.
13. Wheels with two tires on them.

Down

1. The driver uses this to make the truck go faster.
2. The part of the truck that loads the garbage.
3. The metal plate that compacts the garbage.
4. The name of the department that collects trash.
6. The driver uses this to steer the truck.
9. Being squeezed down into a much smaller space.
10. Another name for the gas pedal.

CHAPTER 27

Seashore Environments: *The Seashore Book*

Written by Charlotte Zolotow
New York: HarperCollins, 1992

SUMMARY

A young boy spends an event-filled day at the beach.

RELATED CONCEPTS

The seashore is filled with many interesting plants and animals.

The sea changes its level several times during the day.

The seashore offers lighthouses and other safety devices for mariners.

RELATED VOCABULARY

clam	sandpiper
dune	sea grass
fishing pier	seashore
gull	seaweed
life buoy	shells
lighthouse	snail
moss	tide
oyster	waves
sand crab	

ACTIVITIES

Language Arts

Plan a day at the beach. Two books may help build background information for students who are not familiar with the beach or the ocean: *The Ocean Alphabet Book* by Jerry Palotta and *A Swim through the Sea* by Kristen Joy Pratt.

Web sites can help students decide what they would take for a beach experience. Examples are www.ehow.com/how-6050-pack-trip-beach.html and http://www.fabuloustravel.com/tips/beach.html.

A family of four, two adults and two small children, have allotted $100.00 to outfit themselves for a week at the beach. What can they buy from the following list of items?

Beach umbrella and pole	$15.00
Sunblock lotion	$8.00 for 6 oz. or $12.00 for 12 oz.
Hats	$6.00 or $9.00 or $12.00
Sand pails and shovels	$8.00
Beach Towels	$9.00 or $12.00
Disposable camera	$9.00
Cooler	$15.00

Writing

Imagine taking a trip to the beach, just like the little boy in the book. What would be your favorite activities? What would be your overall feelings about the day? If you have not been to the shore, imagine what a trip would be like.

Social Studies

Locate the national seashores of the United States (see Figure 27.1)—Assateague Island, Maryland, Canaveral, Florida, Cape Cod, Massachusetts, Cape Hatteras, North Carolina, Cape Lookout, North Carolina, Cumberland Island, Georgia, Padre Island, Texas, Point Reyes, California, Gulf Islands, Mississippi/Florida, Fire Island, New York. What is the closest seashore to the students? In which direction would they go to travel there?

Figure 27.1. U.S. map

Science

Two problems that face persons going to the beach are sunburn and dehydration. Think of products that could alleviate both problems and make commercials to advertise these.

Using a hand lens, observe a sample of sea sand. Several different varieties can be selected for comparison purposes—for example, color, size, and texture. What is the origin of these samples of sand? NOTE: Several varieties of beach sand can be ordered at http://www.eBay.com in the "weird stuff" category.

Plant seeds in two different pots—one containing potting soil and one containing sand. Water the seeds. Observe the growth and write down several entries to explain what happened.

Beaches throughout the world may be viewed on the Internet. As many Web cams show live images, teachers will want to review any to be used by classes. May different kinds of beaches can be seen, including some that are experiencing night while the children in the classroom are experiencing day. See, for example, http://www.webcamplaza.net/master_frame_fix.html and http://www.webcamplaza.net/cams/beach.html for an international selection of beaches.

Barrier islands are not permanent. (See Figure 27.2) They can shift position as they absorb the energy of the waves that are crashing against the coast. How does this affect a house being built on one of the barrier islands along the coast of the United States?

To see the effect of waves, build a mound of wet sand in a clear, plastic container. Rhythmically push water against the mound. Eventually the mound will cease to exist and the sand will be scattered over the bottom of the container.

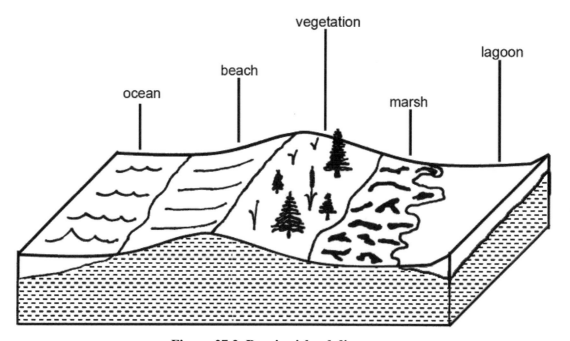

Figure 27.2. Barrier island diagram

Mathematics

Some beaches have a profusion of shells to collect. Collect several shells and put them in categories—for example, cone shaped or snail shaped as well as according to size, color, shape, and texture. Make a graph showing all of the categories of the shells. If sea shells do not exist at the beach, store bought ones can be substituted. NOTE: See http://www.seashells.org/ for information on obtaining seashells.

The Arts

Use the beach coloring pages (Figure 27.3) to help learn the names of beach creatures. Signs are meant to keep beach goers on the paths. Design a sign that says "Keep off the dunes."

Design a sandcastle that can be built at the beach. List any equipment that can be used during this process, and provide a description of the actual process of the building of the castle.

Information Literacy

Animals of the beach will vary from location to location. Some locations provide excellent resources online to explain their beach creatures. One of the best seashell Web guides (http://www.sanibel-captiva.org/play/guide.asp) is from Sanibel Island in Florida. Search the Web for a variety of examples of sea life to be found on beaches that could be visited. Print pictures of sea life for a classroom collection.

REFERENCES

Abbott, R. Tucker, and Herbert S. Zim. *Seashells of the World.* New York: A Golden Guide from St. Martin's Press, 2001.

Douglass, Jackie Leatherbury. *Peterson First Guide to Shells of North America.* New York: Houghton Mifflin, 1998

Palatta, Jerry. *The Ocean Alphabet Book.* Watertown, MA: Charlesbridge Publishers, 1986.

Pratt, Kristen Joy. *A Swim through the Sea.* Nevada City, CA: Dawn Publications, 1994.

Zim, Herbert S., Lester Ingle, and Dorothea Barlowe. *Seashore Life.* New York: A Golden Guide from St. Martin's Press, 2001.

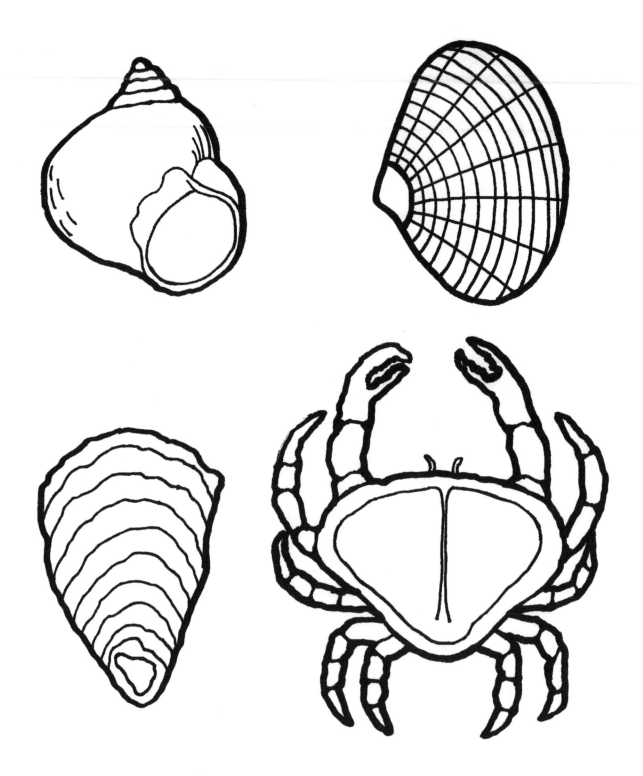

Figure 27.3. Beach coloring pages

The Seashore Book

Across

1. A buoy that helps save lives.
4. Shellfish with two hinged shells.
6. Marine algae—often very large structures.
8. The outer hard parts of animals.
10. Ridges in the water caused by wind.
13. A sand hill made by windblown sand.
15. A wading bird that moves along the coast and eats small organisms from the surf.
16. A shellfish with a spiraled shell.
17. The area where the ocean and the land meet.

Down

2. A delicious shellfish with two irregular shells.
3. Grass that is adapted to living submerged in saltwater.
5. Carpet-like plants.
7. A pier built to assist fishing.
9. A building with a strong light that aids mariners.
11. A small, white crab that hides in small holes in the sand.
12. The regular changes in ocean level during the day.
14. A white/grey seabird with a yellow bill and pink legs.

From *The Natural World Through Children's Literature: An Integrated Approach* by Carol M. Butzow and John W. Butzow. Westport, CT: Libraries Unlimited/Teacher Ideas Press. Copyright © 2007.

Answers to Crossword Puzzles

Mr. Seahorse

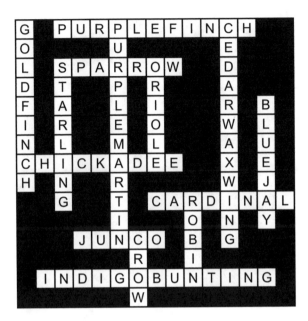

Wild Birds

From Head to Toe

What Do You Do with a Tail Like This?

The Very Ugly Bug

In the Small, Small Pond

Slowly, Slowly, Slowly Said the Sloth

Teeth, Tails, and Tentacles

Meeting Trees

My Brothers' Flying Machine

The Ugly Vegetables

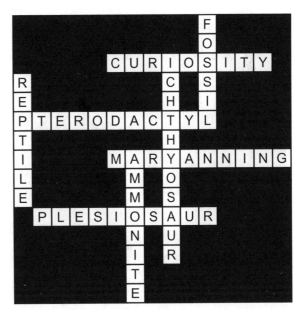

Fossil Girl

M Is for Majestic

The Incredible Water Show
CONDENSATION

The Incredible Water Show
EVAPORATION

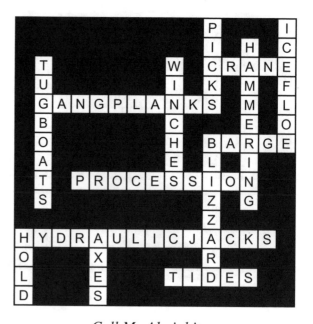

Call Me Ahnighito

Maria's Comet

Twister

The Tortoise and the Jackrabbit

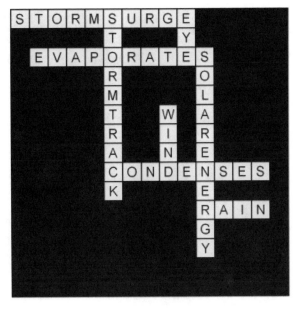

Hurricane

Henry Works

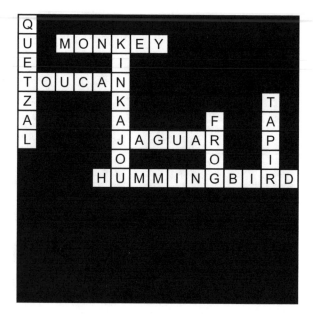

The Umbrella

The Water Hole

How Ben Franklin Stole the Lightning

The Sea, the Storm, and the Mangrove Tangle

I Stink

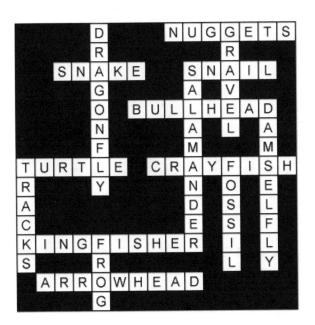

Crawdad Creek

The Seashore Book

Index

About the Authors

Carol and John Butzow live in Indiana, Pennsylvania, where John is a retired education dean and professor of science of education, most recently at Indiana University of Pennsylvania. Carol teaches English as a Second Language to elementary students. For twenty years they have collaborated on well-known books for teachers, including *Science Through Children's Literature, The World of Work Through Children's Literature, Exploring the Environment Tthrough Children's Literature, The American Hero in Children's Literature,* and other titles.

John and Carol have traveled extensively throughout the United States, including Alaska, to present workshops, in-service courses, and conferences. They have also spoken to audiences in Canada, Scotland, and Sweden. For information on workshops or conferences, please contact them through Libraries Unlimited.